Experiencing the Mind of Christ

This Is Going to Blow Your Mind

Theresa Cummings

Trilogy Christian Publishers A Wholly Owned Subsidiary of Trinity Broadcasting Network 2442 Michelle Drive Tustin, CA 92780

First Trilogy Christian Publishing softcover edition December 2018

Trilogy Christian Publishing/ TBN and colophon are trademarks of Trinity Broadcasting Network.

For information about special discounts for bulk purchases, please contact Trilogy Christian Publishing.

Manufactured in the United States of America

10 9 8 7 6 5 4 3 2 1

Library of Congress Cataloging-in-Publication Data is available.

B-ISBN#: 978-1-64088-229-4 E-ISBN#: 978-1-64088-230-0

PROLOGUE

We are living in very exciting times in the Body of Christ as the Spirit of God is moving mightily to tear down divisions, destroy religious strongholds, and release a fresh revelation of our heavenly Father's love for us. There is unparalleled revival around the globe. Additionally, there is a fresh call to understand his desire for us to take on the mind of Christ.

1 Corinthians 2:16 tells us, "For who has understood the mind of the Lord so as to instruct him? But we have the mind of Christ." (NIV) Any believer who knows the word of God is familiar with this scripture, but if you're anything like me, then your mind will be blown away when you realize how accessible the mind of Christ is to us who believe in him , and how little time we have spent seeking to experience it.

As we appropriate the mind of Christ, our new man radiates the love that is God, overpowering the old man and its influence, empowering us to be the love that is God to the world. It is an awe-inspiring journey filled with innumerable surprises and unlimited possibilities. I pray that you will take time to read the words of this book carefully and thoughtfully. This is not for the faint of heart, but for those seeking to accomplish all that God has planned for them, which is far superior to our own plans.

Finally, I am not presenting some type of formula here but sharing from my own journey. The Lord may deal with you somewhat differently, but the word of God remains the standard for us all. My ultimate desire is to see us come into the Spirit of Oneness Christ spoke of in John 17:23. May the word of God have its way in each of our lives.

Theresa Cummings

Proverbs 23:7 "For as he thinks in his heart, so is he."

Chapters

Chapter One

Brain Change

Our very thoughts and perceptions of the world around us, our decisions, and behaviors are initiated in our brains. It operates as the control center of the human body. Without it, our bodies cannot move. All memories reside in our brain center. It is, in fact, the center of our nervous system which coordinates voluntary and involuntary actions. Scientists tell us that there are more neurons in our brain than there are stars in our galaxy, making one million new connections every day. Neurons process everything we see, hear, and experience, as they scurry around connecting new information with old relative information previously stored. The endless stream of incoming information is sorted and categorized in a spectacular orderly frenzy. I get tired just thinking about how busy my brain is.

On the most basic level, as with any other organ of our body, the efficiency of our brain's performance depends on many factors: genetics, environment, nourishment, fitness, and the vast array of experiences we encounter throughout our lives.

Over the last several decades, new scientific discoveries have revealed what once were mysteries of the human brain. Most importantly is the scientific discovery that we can control the activity within the brain and change the course of our thought life. Neuroscientific trials have verified that changing our thoughts can affect our entire physical and emotional experience. This has been a revolutionary discovery of epic proportion.

With permission, I am quoting from the website of Dr. Dan Siegel, world-renowned neurobiology psychiatrist, who plainly states that "....one of the most exciting scientific discoveries of the last twenty years is that how we focus our attention shapes the structure of our brains. Neuroscience has also definitively shown that we can grow these new connections throughout our lives, not just in childhood."

Dr. Siegel is the developer of Mindsight, which helps individuals see the internal workings of their own minds, get off the autopilot of ingrained behaviors and habitual responses. It lets us "name and tame" the emotions we are experiencing, rather than being overwhelmed by them.

Another point of interest is the differences between the physical brain and the non-physical mind. Science has begun to uncover the complex relationship between the two and continues to explore their inter-connectivity. To begin with, the human brain and one's mind are physiologically different.

The brain is a physical component of our body with measurable functions and matter. It has an amazing ability to interpret the information being received moment by moment through our five sensory organs (eyes, ears, nose, tongue, and touch). In fact, different sections of the brain have their own specific functions. For example, basic physical actions such as swallowing, breathing, sneezing, and the beating of the heart are controlled by the brainstem. Furthermore, the section of the brain called the cerebellum coordinates things like our muscle movements, ability to balance our body, and maintain posture. Without getting too far into brain function, suffice it to say that our brains act as the control center of all that we do.

The mind, however, is not an organ, or physical entity. As defined in the Oxford Dictionary, it is "the element of a person that enables them to be aware of the world and their experiences, to think, and to feel; the faculty of consciousness and thought. A person's ability to think and reason; the intellect."

We are not told in scripture to have the "brain" of Christ, but the "mind" of Christ. Although influenced by the vast data stored within the brain, the mind gives us the ability to choose what we think about and how we respond to life. Before moving into how this all relates to experiencing the mind of Christ, I would like to share some meaningful quotes from my favorite author on our ability to change our brain by changing our thinking. In Dr. Caroline Leaf's book *Who Switched Off My Brain?*, she explains how our thought life operates, how thoughts affect our body, and how we can change our thinking. Following are some excerpts from the book that I am sharing with her permission.

"Research shows that around 87% of illnesses can be attributed to our thought life, and approximately 13% to diet, genetics and environment. Studies conclusively link more chronic (also known as lifestyle diseases) to an epidemic of toxic emotions in our culture."

"Quite simply, there is no longer any doubt that what and how you think affect your emotional and physical state. The mind and body are integrally connected."

"There are two important groups of emotions: positive faith-based emotions and negative fear-based emotions. Each of these groups has its own set of emotional molecules attached to it. Faith and fear are not just emotions, but spiritual forces with chemical and electrical representation in the body. Consequently they directly impact bodily function. Every emotion results in an attitude. An attitude is a state of mind that produces a reaction in the body and a resultant behavior."

"All these cerebral parts are interconnected and play a role in creating

a biochemical representation of a thought, processing that thought, building memory and giving thought the emotional and physiological part of your life. These structures are the ones that allow thoughts of peace and serenity to put your body at ease, or fearful thoughts to catapult you into 'fight or flight' mode, with stress hormones coursing through your veins."

"Thoughts that you don't deal with properly become suppressed and can cause emotional and physical harm."

I highly value Dr. Leaf's research and books as she simplifies the scientific data on how our thoughts interact with our brain and ultimately affect our body. Although I have no background in neurosciences, I can conceptualize the cause and effect of thoughts because of her writing. I also read her book *Switch on Your Brain* and will add the following excerpts for your benefit.

"Scientists are finally beginning to see the brain as having renewable characteristics; it is no longer viewed as a machine that is hardwired early in life, unable to adapt, and wearing out with age."

"Matter does not control us; we control matter through our thinking and choosing. We cannot control the events and circumstances of life, but we can control our reactions. In fact, we can control our reactions to anything, and in doing so, we can change our brain. It's not easy; it is hard work, but it can be done through our thoughts and choices. Taking this to a deeper level, research shows that DNA actually changes shape according to our thoughts."

"When you understand the power of your thought life, you truly begin to get a glimpse of how important it is to take responsibility for what you are thinking. Thinking is a powerful and creative force, both a blessing and a curse, and should not be taken lightly."

"Purposefully catching your thoughts can control the brain's sensory processing, the brains rewiring, the neurotransmitters, the genetic

expression, and cellular activity in a positive or negative direction. You choose."

"Getting your thoughts disciplined and under control is one of the first steps in freeing yourself of the burdens of the world and beginning to enjoy life despite the burdens of the world. When you objectively observe your own thinking with the view to capturing rogue thoughts, you in effect direct your attention to stop the negative impact and rewire healthy new circuits into your brain."

"Our thoughts, imaginations, and choices can change the structure and function of our brains on every level: molecular, genetic, epigenetic, cellular, structural, neurochemical, and electromagnetic, and even subatomic. Through our own thoughts, we can be our own brain surgeons as we make choices that change the circuits in our brain. We are designed to do our own brain surgery."

"Your patterns of genetic experience don't determine what you are; you do. How you live, the cultural environment you live in, whatever you immerse yourself in, your beliefs and the beliefs or those around you, how you interact with those people, your faith and how you grow it, what you expose yourself to - all of these lead to differences in the way you focus your attention and have a direct effect on how your proteins are synthesized, how your enzymes act, and how your neurochemicals work together. If you don't believe you have the power to change your thoughts and control your choices, you are not going to do it."

All this information is meant to make known how much power the mind has in relation to brain function and the quality of life experienced through our bodies. It is our responsibility to take control of what we think about, not only to ensure our well-being, but to support the renewal of our minds for spiritual purposes (Romans 12:2).

"The world as we have created it is a process of our thinking. It cannot be changed without changing our thinking." (Albert Einstein)

Chapter Two

It's All in Your Mind

So, now we know that there is scientific evidence proving the pliability of our brains and the important effects our thoughts have on our entire lives. The fact that we can truly renew our minds and develop different thought patterns is a faith igniter for change. It confirms the reality that we can exchange our earthbound way of thinking for a heavenly mindset on a far greater scale than we have known. Although this is great news, it comes with a different set of questions. The largest of them is "Where do I begin?" As with learning any spiritual truths, it begins with God's word and God's heart.

The word of God is alive in incredibly marvelous ways. Most of us are familiar with Hebrews 4:12, "For the word of God is living and powerful, and sharper than any two-edged sword, piercing even to the division of soul and spirit, and of joints and marrow, and is a discerner of the thoughts and intents of the heart." Have you ever read a passage of scripture many times over, but one day read it and gained a much deeper understanding of it? It is truly alive on so many different levels, breathing life and light into our beings. With that said, it's time to dig into the word of God.

Strong's Exhaustive Concordance is an excellent resource for learning the word on a deeper level by reading the original Greek and/or Hebrew of a text. For example, take Romans 12:1-2:

I beseech you therefore, brethren, by the mercies of God, that you present your bodies a living sacrifice, holy, acceptable to God, which is your reasonable service. And do not be conformed to this world, but be transformed by the renewing of your mind, that you may prove what is that good and acceptable and perfect will of God.

There were no surprises with the literal translations within this text until I got to the word *transformed*. The root word for "transformed" (#G3933 Strong's Concordance) is metamorphoō which is the same as our metamorphosis, meaning to change, transfigure, transform. As you may recall from science, butterflies are a common example of metamorphosis. Life begins once the egg becomes a larva and each subsequent stage of growth looks nothing like the adult form of a beautiful butterfly. The process involves phases of development from birth that radically change the internal structure of the being as well as appearance. The transformation creates a new species.

The fact that this is the word used for transformation is amazing. It's only used five times in the Bible and they are all in the New Testament. We are to become entirely different, according to the new creation within us. We should speak differently, act differently, think differently, and live differently. Yet as with metamorphosis, it is a process. Each individual will change at a different pace. We can all speculate why this is the case, but such guessing is simply that: guessing.

2 Corinthians 3:18 says, "But we all, with unveiled face, beholding as in a mirror the glory of the Lord, are being transformed into the same image from glory to glory, just as by the Spirit of the Lord." As we behold him through worship, the word, personal time with him , or within us, we are transformed by the Holy Spirit.

The New Testament is full of examples of those who steadily transformed into Christlikeness and those who kept getting stuck in the old nature, or worse, seduced away from the truth by false doctrine. The early disciples pressed forward into the image of Christ, remaining faithful to the calling to die to self in order that Christ might live in and through them including Paul, Timothy, Peter, John, Silvanus, Silas, Onesimus, Tychicus, Epaphras and Barnabas to name just a few. Others were mentioned as having fallen away from the faith such as Demas, Alexander, Hymenaeus and Philetas (2 Timothy 4:10, 1Timothy 1:19-20, 2 Timothy 2:16-18, 1 Corinthians 5:1-5).

Upon accepting Jesus as our Lord, the Holy Spirit of God takes up residency within us, but he doesn't control us. Each of us is responsible for bringing forth the new creation of Christ within us. Paul explains this as a "putting off" our old selves and "putting on" our new self.

> If indeed you have heard Him and have been taught by Him, as the truth is in Jesus: that you put off, concerning your former conduct, the old man which grows corrupt according to the deceitful lusts, and be renewed in the spirit of your mind, and that you put on the new man which was created according to God, in true righteousness and holiness.

> Therefore, putting away lying, 'Let each one of you speak truth with his neighbor,' for we are members of one another. 'Be angry, and do not sin': do not let the sun go down on your wrath, nor give place to the devil. Let him who stole, steal no longer, but rather let him labor, working with his hands what is good, that he may have something to give him who has need. Let no corrupt word proceed out of your mouth, but what is good for necessary edification, that it may impart grace to the hearers.

> And do not grieve the Holy Spirit of God, by whom you were sealed for the day of redemption. Let all bitterness, wrath, anger, clamor, and evil speaking be put away from you, with

all malice. And be kind to one another, tenderhearted, forgiving one another, even as Christ forgave you.

Ephesians 4:21-32

Paul is very clear in this epistle to the church in Ephesus that we have a responsibility to rid ourselves of the "old man" and take on (or put on) the new nature residing within us. Paul continues this theme throughout chapter five, specifically verses 1-21.

Therefore be imitators of God as dear children. And walk in love, as Christ also has loved us and given Himself for us, an offering and a sacrifice to God for a sweet-smelling aroma. But fornication and all uncleanness or covetousness, let it not even be named among you, as is fitting for saints: neither filthiness, nor foolish talking, nor coarse jesting, which are not fitting, but rather giving of thanks. For this you know, that no fornicator, or unclean person, nor covetous man, who is an idolater, has any inheritance in the kingdom of Christ and God. Let no one deceive you with empty words, for because of these things the wrath of God comes upon the sons of disobedience.

Therefore do not be partakers with them. For you were once darkness, but now you are light in the Lord. Walk as children of light (for the fruit of the Spirit is in all goodness, righteousness, and truth), finding out what is acceptable to the Lord. And have no fellowship with the unfruitful works of darkness, but rather expose them. For it is shameful even to speak of those things which are done by them in secret. But all things that are exposed are made manifest by the light, for whatever makes manifest is light. Therefore He says: 'Awake, you who sleep, Arise from the dead, And Christ will give you light.'

See then that you walk circumspectly, not as fools but as wise, redeeming the time, because the days are evil. Therefore do not be unwise, but understand what the will of the Lord is. And do not be drunk with wine, in which is dissipation: but be filled with the Spirit, speaking to one another in psalms and hymns and spiritual songs, singing and making melody in your heart to the Lord, giving thanks always for all things to God the Father in the name of our Lord Jesus Christ, submitting to one another in the fear of God.

Ephesians 5: 1-21

In his letter to the Romans, Paul also points out what the believer must do away with, reinforcing that we have a crucial part to play in living according to the new nature within us.

The night is far spent; the day is at hand. Therefore let us cast off the works of darkness and let us put on the armor of light. Let us walk properly, as in the day, not in revelry and drunkenness, not in lewdness and lust, not in strife and envy. But put on the Lord Jesus Christ, and make no provision for the flesh, to fulfill its lusts.

Romans 13: 12-14

Ah, the flesh, the fallen flesh. The flesh of our old nature is relentlessly driven by earthly concerns, carnal yearnings, lust and desires, all pointing to satisfying the ego. Yet God has provided us with a way of escape: the Holy Spirit.

I say then: Walk in the Spirit, and you shall not fulfill the lust of the flesh. For the flesh lusts against the Spirit, and the Spirit against the flesh; and these are contrary to one another, so that you do not do the things that you wish. But if you are led by the Spirit, you are not under the law. Now the works of the flesh are evident, which are: adultery, fornication, uncleanness, lewdness, idolatry, sorcery, hatred, contentions, jealousies, outbursts of wrath, selfish ambitions, dissensions, heresies, envy, murders, drunkenness, revelries, and the like; of which I tell you beforehand, just as I told you in time past, that those who practice such things will not inherit the kingdom of God.

Galatians 5:16-21

The more we pursue God, the more we can see how detrimental fleshly desires are to our spiritual growth and we develop a distaste for carnal activity. In other words, as we grow in fellowshipping with the Spirit of Christ within us and regularly reading the word of God, the difference between the old and new becomes increasingly apparent.

As we deepen our friendship with Christ, we are lifted into the spiritual realm he has prepared for us through his life and death on the cross (Ephesians 2:6). The Spirit of Wisdom becomes active within us. This is manifest in our thoughts as we begin to develop an awareness of the Holy Spirit leading us in our actions, feelings, and attitudes.

> For what man knows the things of a man except the spirit of a man which is in him? Even so no one knows the things of God except the Spirit of God. Now we have received, not the spirit of the world, but the Spirit who is from God, that we might know the things that have been freely given to us by God. These things we also speak, not in words which man's wisdom teaches, but which the Holy Spirit teaches, comparing spiritual things with spiritual. But the natural man does not receive the things of the Spirit of God, for they are foolishness to him; nor can he know them for they are spiritually discerned.

1 Corinthians 2:11-14

The difference between the flesh and the Spirit is so extreme, that we are told they are at complete odds with one another.

> For those who live according to the flesh set their minds on the things of the flesh, but those who live according to the Spirit, the things of the Spirit. For to be carnally minded is death, but to be spiritually minded is life and peace. Because the carnal mind is enmity against God; for it is not subject to the law of God, nor indeed can be.
>
> Romans 8:5-7

The Greek translation for enmity is "enemy, hostile." This is a serious contrast and we would be wise to give our attention to such words. Or what about the term is this passage "carnally minded"? I believe we can all agree that a carnal mind thinks less than wholesome thoughts and has sinful attitudes. Yet in Ephesians 4, Paul uses much more graphic language that emphasizes just how ungodly our carnal mind has been, which I have italicized and added brackets.

> This I say, therefore, that you should no longer walk as the rest of the Gentiles walk, in the *futility of their mind*, having their *understanding darkened*, being *alienated from the life of God*, because of the *ignorance* that is in them, because of the *blindness of their heart*; who, *being past feeling (meaning calloused)*, have given themselves over to lewdness, to work all uncleanness with greediness.
>
> Ephesians 4:17-19

We clearly have an old way of thinking as well as the God given opportunity to grow into a radically new way of thinking available to us through Christ. Ephesians 4:23 (NIV) instructs us "to be made new in the attitude of your minds," which is an enormous undertaking. What we used to think about was unprofitable and the mind needs a complete overhaul. On a very practical level, we can begin by simply not going to places that fed our appetite for the things of this world, end friendships that were based on vulgar activity, and stop listening to/looking at things that promoted carnal yearnings. These are all good advancements in putting off the old nature, but we are called to even greater freedom.

As discussed in the previous chapter, we have patterns of behavior that are triggered in our brains that are tied to patterns of thoughts. We are now able to change them on a biological level.

"Therefore, if anyone is in Christ, he is a new creation; old things have passed away; behold, all things have become new." (2 Corinthians 5:17)

Chapter Three

Mind Renewal

As the offspring of Adam and Eve, we are born with a mind that seeks its own way. Such thinking is based on earthly principles orchestrated to serve our own needs and desires. Our brains are full of carnal circuitry that is focused on pleasing self and our neural circuit connections are wired for self-preservation. Yet in Christ, we have the ability to rewire how we think, feel, and react to life on earth, to be who God originally designed us to be. The rewiring process begins by taking control of our thoughts and flooding our minds with the stuff of God's Kingdom.

"For the weapons of our warfare are not carnal but mighty in God for pulling down strongholds, casting down arguments and every high thing that exalts itself against the knowledge of God, bringing every thought into captivity to the obedience of Christ." (2 Corinthians 10:4-5)

Let's begin with the last part of verse 5 here, since it is a very practical way of viewing our thought life: "bringing every thought into captivity to the obedience of Christ." The Greek here implies "taking captive." Captivity is the condition of being imprisoned or confined. Both the words "imprisoned" and "confined" serve us well within the context of taking charge of our thoughts. Simplistically, it is controlling what we think.

As we all know, the mind has a steady stream of thoughts throughout the waking hours. Thoughts even keep some people awake at night. At times, we may even say that our mind is racing. Typically, our thoughts are controlling us without our interference. Our lives radically change when we take control of overflowing thoughts and fill our minds with the things of heaven.

Start your personal exploration by taking one day with a commitment to be aware of your thoughts and observe what you're thinking about. No fudging here! You need to be genuinely honest. Consider how much time is spent thinking about the *past*, about the *future*, about the *Lord*, or about *yourself*. Surprising, isn't it? At first, just one day in this process can be exhausting from the energy it takes to monitor one's thought life. Most people aren't accustomed to this activity and it takes great effort.

The *past* is often a stronghold in our minds, torturing us with thoughts of past failures, past pain, or even past relationships. These thoughts are futile and a waste of time and mental energy. They work against our faith and weaken us spiritually and physically. I have often told myself, "Don't look back; you're not going that way."

"Do not remember the former things, nor consider the things of old." (Isaiah 43:18)

"No one who puts a hand to the plow and looks back is fit for service in the Kingdom of God." (Luke 9:62)

"Brethren, I do not count myself to have apprehended; but one thing I do, forgetting those things which are behind and reaching forward to those things which are ahead, I press toward the goal for the prize of the upward call of God in Christ Jesus." (Phil. 3:13-14)

Although we don't want to be focused on the negative events of our past, we are encouraged to remember the faithfulness of God within our life history.

"I remember the days of old; I meditate on all your works; I muse on the work of your hands." (Psalm 143:5)

"I will remember the works of the Lord; Surely I will remember Your wonders of old." (Psalm 77:11)

Despite the pain in our past, God can use it to help others in their time of need.

"And we know that all things work together for good to those who love God, to those who are called according to His purpose." (Romans 8:28) It is not uncommon to encourage others by sharing what God has brought us through in the past.

> Blessed be the God and Father of our Lord Jesus Christ, the Father of mercies and God of all comfort, who comforts us in all our tribulation, that we may be able to comfort those who are in any trouble, with the comfort with which we ourselves are comforted by God.
>
> 2 Corinthians 1: 3-4

In this way, we can remember things from our past that relate to God's faithfulness, past blessings, and past answers to prayer that are useful for our personal edification and the encouragement of others.

Concerning thinking about the *future*, it's hard to resist since we live in a culture that promotes preparing for the future. The fact of the matter is, not one of us knows what tomorrow may bring. If we can just believe the following words of Jesus, we can recognize the futility of being concerned about the future and trust God in all things.

Therefore do not worry, saying, 'What shall we eat?' or 'What shall we drink?' or 'What shall we wear?' For after all these things the Gentiles seek. For your heavenly Father knows that you need all these things. But seek first the kingdom of God and His righteousness, and all these things shall be added to you. Therefore do not worry about tomorrow, for tomorrow will worry about its own things. Sufficient for the day is its own trouble.

Matthew 6:31-34

How often did you think about the *Lord* during your first day of observation? My common thought about God on that first day was Lord, *I'm really going to need a lot of help with this!* I prayed every day for the Holy Spirit to help me control my thoughts. When I would catch a useless or negative thought, I began speaking to my mind, out loud at times, "No, I reject that thought." The more I rejected thoughts that were against faith, the easier it was to cut them off. I even got to the point of just shaking my head no, which must've looked strange to others around me! I realized it was up to me to take captive every thought that was keeping me preoccupied with the world, distracting me from staying spiritually focused.

Obviously, we have thoughts about life on earth that are necessary for living here, such as getting to work on time, grocery shopping, caring for our children, paying bills on time, and the basic time we must spend thinking on such things in order to function. What we're addressing are thoughts that add no value to our growth into Christlikeness. This isn't rocket science. It's brain science. If you grew up never having enough food, your repeated experience has trained your brain to flood your mind with anxious thoughts if the cupboard is getting empty. Or perhaps it's resulted in a pantry that could provide food for a small village.

Such patterns have been wired into our brains through repeated experiences, reactions and feelings.

In addition to our general thoughts, many people have a difficult time dealing with what is called "self-talk" as in what we say to ourselves about ourselves. How we think about ourselves comes from a very complex system of what we've been told by parents, relatives, friends, and social peers. Unfortunately, the large majority of it weighs in on the negative side such as "Stop being so lazy," "Why can't you be a better student?" "You're so weird," "You're a loser," "When are you going to get it together?" "What's wrong with you?" "You're a mess," and the like. Depending how early in life the berating starts, these words will shape self-perceptions.

It's become a theme in this era regarding bullying at schools and on social media platforms. Bullying among students is at an all-time high in our school systems. Where bullying was once carried out on a playground or was spread through rumors in school, it is now being conducted on social media where the perpetrator can remain anonymous and is free to be as hurtful as possible. According to studies by Yale University, bullying victims are between 2 to 9 times more likely to consider suicide than non-victims. This makes it clear that parents need to go out of their way to speak words of affirmation to their children.

It's important that we recognize that any negative thoughts we have against ourselves is against faith and against Christ as mentioned in 2 Corinthians 10:5, "bringing every thought into captivity to the obedience of Christ."

I am reminded of the now deceased Dr. William Backus. Both a clinical psychologist and minister, he wrote several books including *Self-Talk* and *Telling Yourself the Truth*. For most of us, we have emotions regarding the negative labels we've been living with and I appreciate the way he explained such experiences. The website ministryhealth.net provides important quotes from Dr. Backus books and offers guidance for dealing with destructive self-talk. I highly recommend you read the article Telling Yourself the Truth by Rev. Wayne Dobratz on the website.

"Our emotions are not created by what happens to us; rather, our emotions are created by what we tell ourselves about what happens to us."

"It is not what people say or do that creates your emotions, but rather what you tell yourself about what people say or do to you."

Dr. Backus developed what he coined "Misbelief Therapy," misbelief being a lie that you tell yourself.

"The constant repeating of misbeliefs is what sustains and perpetuates angry resentment. Constant repeating of the truth generates health and peace."

The goal is to consistently be aware of your thoughts, catch the negative ones, reject them, and replace them with positive spiritual thoughts. Consider it training, as in training your body through exercise.

We don't run a marathon if we're out of shape, but we start by walking and then walking farther and then faster. Eventually we'll tackle a light jog to a stronger jog until we finally have developed our muscles and lung capacity to run.

Using this analogy, we start with incremental thought control and work up to the point of continual thought awareness. With practice, controlling our thoughts becomes a consistent activity. Like riding a bike, once you learn it, you never forget it. The best news is that it truly works to renew our minds. As we confront the lies and repeat the truth, our emotions are realigned, and we experience freedom from our old man.

"Then Jesus said to those Jews who believed Him, "If you abide in My word, you are My disciples indeed. And you shall know the truth, and the truth shall make you free." (John 8:31-32)

Besides thinking poorly of ourselves, it helps to consider how often we have negative thoughts in general. Some people are eternal pessimists. They always see what's wrong in a situation, or what's not to their liking. Unfortunately, if our childhood was spent around such people, we pick up their way of thinking as our brains are developing. After all, some pessimistic thoughts make sense like "if you expect the worst, you'll never be disappointed." Or "don't get too happy since something always goes wrong." We're all familiar with the idiom about people who "see the glass half empty instead of half full," or "waiting for the other shoe to drop."

We are called to be eternal optimists, emphasis on the word "eternal." As Christians, our citizenship is in heaven (Philippians 3:20). Jesus said "They are not of this world, just as I am not of the world" in John 17:16. In Christ, all of our excuses for being negative are gone. Not a negative word should cross our lips, but when they do, we need to observe such negative thoughts, refuse to speak them, and figure out what the source is so we pull it out by the roots. Sadly, we are having to buck the worldly system that thrives on complaining and even justifies complaints. People love to say things like "Well she said this," and "They did that," or "Why aren't they talking to me?" and 'How can they be that way?' or "I'm really hurt." Just writing about it nauseates me. This is all carnal foolishness which wastes our time and energy that is meant to be used serving God and others. We are born again to be different from the world. If we still complain, it's evidence that we are still self-centered.

"Beware of harking back to what you once were when God wants you to be something you have never been." (Oswald Chambers)

Chapter Four

The Heart of the Matter

Proverbs 4:23 states "Keep your *heart* with all diligence, for out of it spring the issues of life."

The word "heart" is mentioned in the King James Bible 830 times in 762 verses. It is a core part of our being that is meant to echo the heart of God. Following are some of the most poignant verses related to the spiritual heart.

"You shall love the Lord your God with all your *heart*, with all your soul, and with all your strength." (Deuteronomy 6:5)

"But the word is very near you, in your mouth and in your *heart*, that you may obey it." (Deuteronomy 30:14)

"For the Lord does not see as man sees; for man looks at the outward appearance, but the Lord looks at the *heart*." (1 Samuel 16:7)

"Then I will give them one heart, and I will put a new spirit within them, and take the stony *heart* out of their flesh, and give them a *heart* of flesh." (Ezekiel 11:19)

"For out of the abundance of the *heart* the mouth speaks." (Matthew 12:34b)

"Did not our *heart* burn within us while He talked with us on the road, and while He opened the Scriptures to us?" (Luke 24:32)

"Let not your *heart* be troubled; you believe in God, believe also in Me." (John 14:1)

"So continuing daily with one accord in the temple, and breaking bread from house to house, they ate their food with gladness and simplicity of *heart*." (Acts 2:46)

"For with the *heart* one believes unto righteousness, and with the mouth confession is made unto salvation." (Romans 10:10)

"And thus the secrets of his *heart* are revealed; and so, falling down on his face, he will worship God and report that God is truly among you." (1 Corinthians 14:25)

"Now the purpose of the commandment is love from a pure *heart*, from a good conscience, and from sincere faith." (1 Timothy 1:5)

"Rather let it be the hidden person of the *heart*, with the incorruptible beauty of a gentle and quiet spirit, which is very precious in the sight of God." (1 Peter 3:4)

After reading these scriptures, it's apparent we have a place within our being that is a central part of who we are. It has emotions, thoughts, intentions, and attitudes which are either evil or good. Words such as hard, perverse, evil, wicked, and condemning are all mentioned in the scriptures as conditions of a heart without God.

The part of our brain that most resembles the heart described in the Bible is the limbic system. Composed of several structures, the amygdala, hippocampus, and hypothalamus are considered the main limbic structures and the thalamus feeds the limbic system with sensory input. The purpose of this part of the brain emulates the biblical description of the heart. I will be using the description from the book *The Church: Helping or Hurting?* by Michael Dye, Certified Alcohol and Drug Addiction Counselor. He is the founder of the Genesis Process which guides people struggling with addictions to deal with the core problems found in the limbic system. Not only has Michael given his life to helping addicts, as a Christian he has also focused his time helping churches become a safe place for wounded people.

"The limbic system is located at the center of our brain. It is involved with our deepest beliefs and emotions. It controls our experiential memories, emotions, unconscious emotional learning, dreaming, attention, and our ability to feel pleasure and reward. The limbic system controls arousal and the expression of emotional, motivational, sexual, and social behavior, including the formation of loving attachments."

Michael Dye goes so far as to call the limbic system the seat of the scriptural heart. Although I tend to agree with him, what matters most is that the activities within the limbic system are important when seeking to renew the mind. Following is an excerpt from his Genesis Process workbook used to educate those pursuing freedom from past ungodly thoughts and patterns.

"The limbic system doesn't have a memory like the neocortex. It doesn't know the difference between yesterday and 30 years ago, which explains why some of our childhood traumas still trigger us so powerfully today. It is the limbic system that is most affected by our beliefs, behaviors, and addictions. The limbic system can be negatively programmed through traumatic experiences such as growing up in a dysfunctional family."

"Even though you've discovered false beliefs, uncovered the lies and know a new truth, there is a time lag between what your limbic system believes and what your neocortex has learned. This is called limbic lag, a process that can be anywhere from a couple of months to years, but it will get shorter as you continue to challenge the false beliefs (traumatic memories) and risk trusting people. You may have fear and panic attacks, but once you go through them without doing the old behavior, your limbic system will say, 'Oh, we went through that and actually survived.' The next time you experience the fear it will be less, and you will be able to make a good choice rather than overreacting with a 'fight or flight' response."

"Old automatic habits aren't changed quickly or easily and are stronger when we're tired. Many recovering addicts and trauma survivors have programmed the survival part of their brains with thousands and thousands of instances of avoiding unwanted thoughts or emotions choosing not to 'fight' with their issues, but to take 'flight' into their addiction. Over time, this 'flight' pattern becomes an automatic reaction. With a new identity based on new beliefs, they can change that flight pattern or reprogram their limbic system."

"Change happens one decision at a time. No matter what your emotions tell you would feel good to do (drugs, alcohol, sex, food), listen to what your mind knows, and do what is best or right. If you continue to apply this key thought, you will begin to break the 'flight' pattern and decrease the time of the limbic lag process."

The limbic system within us has been programmed since birth through experiences, many of them having a negative message attached. However, as we spiritually engage in the renewing of our minds, new positive experiences will override the old negative ones that have ruled us for years. It is a matter of persistence and repetition.

According to the scriptures, we need a change of heart. We come to Christ from a position of being closed-hearted; a place in which we are protecting all that we are (the good and the bad) because it's all we've got and we're in charge of it. No one really knows us when we're living to protect our identity. In most cases, we don't even know who we really are.

Once we receive Jesus, we are to be openhearted, living our lives in transparency with nothing to hide or protect. If you want to see how false your life has been, try being transparent with people, as in be honest about your life. In other words, it's time to come out of the closet of deceit and, yes, it is painful, but it is a forerunner to experiencing the mind of Christ. How can we join ourselves to the mind of truth if we ourselves are still in deceit?

When we are closed-hearted, we are often deceitful just because we don't want to be seen as wrong or uninformed, due to our insecurities. This is carried into our spiritual experience. Unfortunately, it is common to hear of a believer, even a pastor at times, that has secretly been practicing evil behavior and when it comes to light everyone is shocked. Come to think of it, I guess the only thing Jesus didn't demonstrate to us when he was on earth was how to admit to someone you were wrong. Nonetheless, he demonstrated the utmost humility, which is certainly required in order to be honest.

The scriptures instruct us to help one another along as we seek to align the attitudes and feelings of our spiritual heart with the openhearted way of Christ.

"Now we exhort you, brethren, warn those who are unruly, comfort the fainthearted, uphold the weak, be patient with all. See that no one renders evil for evil to anyone, but always pursue what is good both for yourselves and for all." (1 Thessalonians 5:14-15)

"All Scripture is given by inspiration of God, and is profitable for doctrine, for reproof, for correction, for instruction in righteousness, that the man of God may be complete, thoroughly equipped for every good work." (2 Timothy 3:16-17)

"Whoever loves instruction loves knowledge, but he who hates correction is stupid." (Proverbs 12:1)

"I will give you a new heart and put a new spirit within you; I will take the heart of stone out of your flesh and give you a heart of flesh." (Ezekiel 36:26)

We're having to adjust to a much bigger heart than the one we've had. Our new heart is full of compassion, tenderness, kindness, patience, and mercy. I remember experiencing the enormity of God's loving heart and saw my heart being so very tiny and, well, dried up. As we get to know God by spending time talking to him and listening for his voice, our heart expands into love, mercy, and grace and we begin to see others with the kindness of God himself. The people of the world are longing to see genuine, authentic believers.

What is most remarkable is the fact that God also has this spiritual heart.

"And the Lord was sorry that He had made man on the earth, and He was grieved in His *heart*." (Genesis 6:6)

"For the day of vengeance is in My *heart*, And the year of My redeemed has come." (Isaiah 63:4)

"And I will give you shepherds according to My *heart*, who will feed you with knowledge and understanding." (Jeremiah 3:15)

"Yes, I will rejoice over them to do them good, and I will assuredly plant them in this land, with all My *heart* and with all My soul." (Jeremiah 32:41)

"Take My yoke upon you and learn from Me, for I am gentle and lowly in *heart*, and you will find rest for your souls." (Matthew 11:29)

We've yet to have much understanding of what it means to be

made in his image (Genesis 1:27) and it appears that we won't understand it until we are in his presence in heaven. Yet it is still amazing to see how we have Godlike capacities that he originally intended for us to fully experience before the fall of Adam and Eve. May we seek to experience them now.

"Prayer is not asking. It is a longing of the soul. It is a daily admission of one's weakness. It is better in prayer to have a heart without words, than words without a heart." (Mahatma Gandhi)

Chapter Five

Conspiracy of Lies

It is important to understand that with our pursuit of the mind of Christ, we are treading on territory that is of the utmost importance to Satan. Satan really isn't so interested in us as individuals, but rather he is vehemently opposed to us becoming Christlike. Be prepared for battle.

Satan is the father of all lies and he does not want us to wake up to who we truly are in Christ but wants to keep us in the lie of our former selves.

When Jesus was in a discourse with the Pharisees, who didn't know what darkness covered their religious minds, he told them:

> You are of your father the devil, and the desires of your father you want to do. He was a murderer from the beginning, and does not stand in the truth, because there is no truth in him. When he speaks a lie, he speaks from his own resources, for he is a liar and the father of it.

> John 8:44

All thoughts running through the mind that are against our position in Christ are the lies of Satan. The mind is Satan's battlefield, so as we begin to take control of our thoughts, we can expect resistance. It's not surprising to experience some random carnal thoughts to distract us from becoming Christlike. As such, the importance of gaining control over our thought life is supreme. "For we are not unaware of his schemes." (2 Corinthians 2:11b)

There is a demonic trinity that effectively quenches faith: fear, worry, and anxiety. All three are based on mistrusting God. Satan used the same tactic to seduce Eve in the garden. It's important to recognizing that Satan caused her to question God, which resulted in her mistrusting God and doubting his goodness.

> Now the serpent was more cunning than any beast of the field which the Lord God had made. And he said to the woman, "Has God indeed said, 'You shall not eat of every tree of the garden'?" And the woman said to the serpent, "We may eat the fruit of the trees of the garden; but of the fruit of the tree which is in the midst of the garden, God has said, 'You shall not eat it, nor shall you touch it, lest you die.'" Then the serpent said to the woman, "You will not surely die. For God knows that in the day you eat of it your eyes will be opened, and you will be like God, knowing good and evil.
>
> Genesis 3:1-5

It is the word of God that defeats Satan's attacks. All he has to destroy our faith is lies, and the truth of God's word is the sword that destroys them. Following are scriptures for refuting the lies that foster fear, worry, and anxiety. I would write them out and hang them on my wall, so I could speak them aloud.

Fear

"The Lord is on my side; I will not fear. What can man do to me?" (Psalm 118:6)

"For you did not receive the spirit of bondage again to fear, but you received the Spirit of adoption by whom we cry out 'Abba, Father.'" (Romans 8:15)

Abba=Papa in the verse above.

"For God has not given us a spirit of fear, but of power and of love and of a sound mind." (2 Timothy 1:7)

"For I, the Lord your God, will hold your right hand, saying to you, 'Fear not, I will help you.'" (Isaiah 41:13)

"Do not be afraid; only believe." (Mark 5:36)

"I sought the LORD, and he heard me, and delivered me from all my fears." (Psalms 34:4)

"So we say with confidence, 'The Lord is my helper; I will not be afraid. What can man do to me?'" (Hebrews 13:6)

Worry

> Therefore I tell you, do not worry about your life, what you will eat or drink; or about your body, what you will wear. Is not life more than food, and the body more than clothes? Look at the birds of the air; they do not sow or reap or store away in barns, and yet your heavenly Father feeds them. Are you not much more valuable than they? Can any one of you by worrying add a single hour to your life?

> And why do you worry about clothes? See how the flowers of the field grow. They do not labor or spin. Yet I tell you that not even Solomon in all his splendor was dressed like one of these. If that is how God clothes the grass of the field, which is here today, and tomorrow is thrown into the fire, will he not much more clothe you—you of little faith? So do not worry, saying, 'What shall we eat?' or 'What shall we drink?' or 'What shall we wear?' For the pagans run after all these things, and your heavenly Father knows that you need them.

> Matthew 6:25-32

"But seek first his kingdom and his righteousness, and all these things will be given to you as well. Therefore do not worry about tomorrow, for tomorrow will worry about itself. Each day has enough trouble of its own." (Matthew 6:33-34)

Anxiety

"In the multitude of my anxieties within me, your comforts delight my soul." (Psalm 94:19)

"Cast all your anxiety on Him, for He cares for you." (1 Peter 5:7 NIV)

"Be anxious for nothing, but in everything by prayer and supplication, with thanksgiving, let your requests be made known to God; and the peace of God, which surpasses all understanding, will guard your hearts and minds through Christ Jesus." (Philippians 4:6-7)

From my personal point of view, I see worry as a smoldering version of fear. Where fear can hit you with strong feelings, worry is an ongoing uneasiness that makes the mind foggy with earthly concerns. I consider anxiety a physical response to frightening potentials. Without being an expert on these psychological states, suffice it to say that all three of them are anti-faith. I believe we can all agree on that.

When we sense fear, worry, or anxiety rising in us, we should evaluate what thought(s) caused it, so we understand what makes us vulnerable to it. We all have "buttons" from the past that Satan knows about. He seeks to push those buttons in order to quench our faith. At such times we need to rebuke Satan, rebuke the thoughts pertaining to such feelings, and reclaim our rightful position of peace in God's loving hands.

"Therefore, preparing your minds for action, and being sober-minded, set your hope fully on the grace that will be brought to you at the revelation of Jesus Christ." (1 Peter 1:13)

These words of the Apostle Peter confirm the need for us to get our mind in a position of readiness, trusting in the grace of our Lord to reveal his will for us.

We serve a God who cannot lie. All his words are true.

"This truth gives them confidence that they have eternal life, which God—who does not lie—promised them before the world began." (Titus 1:2 NLT)

Once again, we need to recognize that it's only as we accept a thought on a repeated basis that it gains power in our brains. For people who have lived a long time with fear, worry, and anxiety, there are pathways in the brain that have strong memories and are well established. It's easy to get discouraged when we have persistent impulses, feelings, and thoughts associated with negativity. Yet this is not insurmountable, it just takes longer and requires a more focused effort of rejecting such feelings and thoughts and repeating scriptures that prove they're lies.

"The secret of living a life of excellence is merely a matter of thinking thoughts of excellence. Really, it's a matter of programming our minds with the kind of information that will set us free." (Charles R. Swindoll)

Chapter Six

Put on Light

"The night is nearly over; the day is almost here. So let us put aside the deeds of darkness and put on the armor of light." (Romans 13:12)

Finally, be strong in the Lord and in his mighty power. Put on the full armor of God, so that you can take your stand against the devil's schemes. For our struggle is not against flesh and blood, but against the rulers, against the authorities, against the powers of this dark world and against the spiritual forces of evil in the heavenly realms.

Therefore put on the full armor of God, so that when the day of evil comes, you may be able to stand your ground, and after you have done everything, to stand. Stand firm then, with the belt of truth buckled around your waist, with the breastplate of righteousness in place, and with your feet fitted with the readiness that comes from the gospel of peace. In addition to all this, take up the shield of faith, with which you can extinguish all the flaming arrows of the evil one. Take the helmet of salvation and the sword of the Spirit, which is the word of God.

And pray in the Spirit on all occasions with all kinds of prayers and requests. With this in mind, be alert and always keep on praying for all the Lord's people.

Ephesians 6:10-18

Most believers are familiar with this important section of the word of God, but they don't realize it as an important focus of each day to strengthen our inner man. No part of our spiritual gear has been left out. Nonetheless, it is only as we mature as a disciple that we can understand the importance of this armor. At each level of our growth, the substance and vital role of each piece of armor expands significantly. Mature believers grow in their understanding of the scriptures.

Since our battle is not with flesh and blood, spiritual warfare requires a determination that nothing will prevent us from living according to the will of God for our lives. The armor is already victorious against darkness, but it doesn't just magically appear on us, we must put it on.

The belt of truth establishes us as sincere believers in the sacrifice of Christ on our behalf. In John 17:17, Jesus said, "Sanctify them by your truth; your word is truth." Since the belt in the armor holds all other pieces in place, it is essential that we become people of the word: read it, listen to it, meditate on it during the day and night. Psalm 119:105 says, "Your word is a lamp for my feet, a light on my path." Psalm 119:15 also says ,"I meditate on your precepts and consider your ways."

"Therefore you shall lay up these words of mine in your heart and in your soul, and bind them as a sign on your hand, and they shall be as frontlets between your eyes." (Deuteronomy 11:18) The original command for the term "frontlets" was used figuratively for "perpetual remembrance" (Brown-Driver-Briggs Hebrew and Aramaic Lexicon).

The breastplate of righteousness is our belief that the righteousness of Christ envelops us, which protects us from judgment, guilt, and shame related to our sin. The role of an actual breastplate is to protect the vital organs of the body, including the heart. Satan wants us to feel guilty, shameful, and unworthy so that faith in the righteousness of Christ would be rendered ineffective.

"For He made Him who knew no sin to be sin for us, that we might become the righteousness of God in Him." (2 Corinthians 5:21)

Having our feet fitted with the readiness that comes from the gospel of peace has to do with the gospel that provides us with peace, knowing that Christ has overcome the world and we can live with a peace that passes human understanding (Philippians 4:7, John 14:27). Being grounded in this truth keeps us supported by the peace provided through what Jesus suffered, so that we are not unnerved by what transpires in life. The enemy wants to create unrest so that our faith wavers. Being "surefooted" in peace cuts off Satan's attempts to get us "out of step" as it were, with lies of fear, worry, and anxiety.

The shield of faith is used to deflect the flaming arrows of Satan. He wants us to doubt God's faithfulness and weaken our confidence in who we are in Christ. Faith is all about our belief system and Satan seeks to challenge that in order to destroy our faith in God. His attacks come in many forms during times of hardship, overwhelming circumstances, and crisis. It is during such life experiences that Satan attacks our confidence in God's goodness and promises to us. As we actively seek God and keep our faith alive, the flaming arrows of the enemy are quenched.

The helmet of salvation protects our thought life. The helmet is an unwavering presence of mind that we have been saved from the condemnation associated with our past lives and are being led by our Father into a life of expectant victory and joy. Simply put, we need to have a clear knowledge of the gospel: what we've been saved *from*, as well as what we've been saved *to*. Such is the essence of salvation that protects our minds from the lies of Satan.

It's fascinating that all our armor is defensive except for the sword of the Spirit, which is an offensive weapon, that being the word of God. As Jesus demonstrated when he was attacked by Satan after his forty-day fast, a single text that is understood and rightly applied sends Satan fleeing (Matthew 4: 1-11). The wisdom of Jesus in his responses is amazingly clear. May we all grow to become so skilled in God's word!

"Do your best to present yourself to God as one approved, a worker who does not need to be ashamed and who correctly handles the word of truth." (2 Timothy 2:15 NIV)

"For the word of God is alive and active. Sharper than any double-edged sword, it penetrates even to dividing soul and spirit, joints and marrow; it judges the thoughts and attitudes of the heart." (Hebrews 4:12)

As mentioned previously, the word of God is alive and a valuable defense against Satan. He hates the word of God and will retreat when we speak it against him. To do this, we must know it. Read the Bible as much as possible and get to *know* the word so you can rebuke the lies of Satan and make him flee. If it worked for Jesus, it will work for us.

Most important is how this section of scripture ends. All parts of the armor are fastened together through prayer. This one verse is powerful and essential to our success during battles.

"And pray in the Spirit on all occasions with all kinds of prayers and requests. With this mind, be alert and always keep on praying for all the Lord's people." (Ephesians 6:18)

Without getting into a commentary about this passage and praying in the Holy Spirit, suffice it to say that God alone enables us not only to fight spiritual warfare, but he alone gives us victory over our enemies. Recognizing our complete dependence on him, a lifestyle of prayer is crucial.

We're told in 1 Thessalonians 5:17 to "pray without ceasing." Obviously, we can't do this if we believe prayer is a posture or formulated words. Prayer extends far beyond such concepts. It is a spiritual awareness of his continual presence within us, "Christ in you, the hope of glory." (Colossians 1:27, Romans 8: 10-11)

Communing with his heart throughout the day with thoughts of thanksgiving and worship are forms of prayer, as well as entreating him on behalf of others or simply talking to him as our Father. It's about living from a place of mindfulness, acknowledging his presence regardless of what we are doing. Growing into continual prayer is a process that naturally flows as we become more mature in Christ.

A good example is in John 15, when Jesus was teaching his disciples about "abiding in him," using the example of a vineyard. Christ is the vine and we are the branches and he tells us that, "If you abide in Me and My words abide in you, you will ask what you desire, and it shall be done for you." (John 15:7) If we are to abide, we need to remain aware of his presence being with us always.

Jesus also made clear the importance of having times of undistracted prayer in our Father's presence. Although he was in continual communication with his Father, he prioritized having time alone with God.

"But Jesus often withdrew to lonely places and prayed." (Luke 5:16)

"Who, in the days of His flesh, when He had offered up prayers and supplication, with vehement cries and tears, and was heard because of His godly fear." (Hebrews 6:7)

"And when He had sent the multitudes away, He went up on the mountain by Himself to pray. Now when evening came, He was alone there." (Matthew 14:23)

"After bidding them farewell, He left for the mountain to pray." (Mark 6:46)

"It was at this time that He went off to the mountain to pray, and He spent the whole night in prayer to God." (Luke 6:12)

"In the early morning, while it was still dark, Jesus got up, left the house, and went away to a secluded place, and was praying there." (Mark 1:35)

"But Jesus Himself would often slip away to the wilderness and pray." (Luke 5:16)

When I think of Jesus communing with his Heavenly Father, it must have been an amazing exchange. As Jesus said, he spoke no words except that which his Father told him to. Mind boggling at the least. How awesome to think of our Father giving us words to speak.

"When you are brought before the synagogues, rulers, and authorities, do not worry about how to defend yourselves or what to say. For at that time the Holy Spirit will teach you what you should say." (Luke 12:11-12)

"However, when He, the Spirit of truth has come, He will guide you into all truth; for He will not speak on His own authority, but whatever He hears He will speak; and He will tell you things to come." (John 16:13)

Herein lies the mystery of the Holy Trinity. Both the Holy Spirit and Jesus do not operate independent of the Father, for they are not rival deities but are one.

"For I have not spoken on my own authority, but the Father who

sent Me, gave Me a command, what I should say and speak."
(John 12:49)

"Do you not believe that I am in the Father and the Father in Me?
The words that I speak to you I do not speak on my own authority;
but the Father who dwells in me does the works." (John 14:10)

May we seek to become one with him and one with each other.

"Let your light so shine before men, that they may see your good
works and glorify your Father in heaven." (Matthew 5:16)

"For you were once darkness, but now you are light in the Lord. Walk as children of the light …" (Ephesians 5:8)

Chapter Seven

Walking Circumspectly

"See then that you walk circumspectly, not as fools but as wise, redeeming the time, because the days are evil. Therefore, do not be unwise, but understand what the will of the Lord is." (Ephesians 5:15-17)

Once we sense we have some degree of control over our thought life, emotions, and reactions to circumstances, we can then begin penetrating even deeper into our spiritual destiny by learning to walk circumspectly. This requires even more self-discipline but produces greater joy as we become increasingly aware of God's kingdom and presence in our lives. Following are some disciplines that require our attention.

Calculated Hearing

This may sound like a strange concept to you, but how we hear is important to Jesus and needs to be important to us. It's easier to understand as "how well we listen." It's not about our auditory hearing, but about thoughtful hearing.

When Jesus told the parable of the sower, his disciples later asked him to explain it to them and it was all about how we hear the word of God.

The sower sows the word. And these are the ones by the

wayside where the word is sown. When they hear, Satan comes immediately and takes away the word that was sown in their hearts. These likewise are the ones sown on stony ground who, when they hear the word, immediately receive it with gladness; and they have no root in themselves, and so endure only for a time. Afterward, when tribulation or persecution arises for the word's sake, immediately they stumble.

Now these are the ones sown among thorns; they are the ones who hear the word, and the cares of this world, the deceitfulness of riches, and the desire for other things entering in choke the word, and it becomes unfruitful. But these are the ones sown on good ground, those who hear the word, accept it, and bear fruit: some thirtyfold, some sixty, and some a hundred.

Mark 4:14-20

Then he added, 'Pay close attention to what you hear. The closer you listen, the more understanding you will be given—and you will receive even more. To those who listen to my teaching, more understanding will be given. But for those who are not listening, even what little understanding they have will be taken away from them.'

Mark 4:24-25 (NLV)

Any Greek exposition will basically convey the same; the Greek's intent is that how well we listen to and think about the spiritual words we hear, the more our spiritual understanding will increase. Conversely, the less attention we give to what the word is saying to us, then the less we will understand it.

Seems like a reasonable concept, but we seem to have a huge infestation of thorny ground in the Western world. Be careful how you receive the word of God, taking time to digest it and live by its directives.

In addition to how we hear or listen to God's words, we also need to be disciplined in how we hear or listen to what others say. Unfortunately, we easily believe what others say without giving it much thought or verifying what we're told.

I was once working for a woman by packing boxes at her home. The television was on and I was watching Joseph Prince preaching. The woman told me I shouldn't watch him because he taught error. I asked why she thought that, and the response was that someone had told her.

This is just one example of a plethora of such instances where some Christians listen to what others say without checking it out. Such activity is commonplace among believers and should not be so. It is gossip, which God detests. When Solomon listed six things that God hates in Proverbs 6:16-19, the last two of the six related to gossip found in verse 19, "a false witness who speaks lies, and one who sows discord among brethren."

Just because someone we may like, love, or respect tells us something doesn't mean we should believe it to be true. This is particularly true when it comes to someone telling us something about another believer or ministry. Such communication is against Christ.

We also hear through our eyes, as in what we're reading and how we respond to it. I once received a lengthy text that was accusatory and judgmental. I had to choose how to react and my brain was already programmed from a life of experiences to get emotionally charged, angry, and defensive. I was able to capture my thoughts and emotions and reject them. Although my negative response kept reemerging for hours, I was able to consistently reject the thoughts and feelings. This process went on the entire evening and even continued the next morning, but the brain signal was weakening. It became an even fainter signal with my continued rejection and finally went away. I was more irritated that it took so long to reverse the brain's automated reaction, but such is the stuff of changing our thought processes.

Since each person's brain is different, being crafted by individual experiences, we need to carefully listen when others speak to us and filter our hearing through godliness, discerning between what is good and what is evil (Hebrews 5:14).

Pay close attention to what you hear from others, what you read, and how well you listen to God's word.

"For though by this time you ought to be teachers, you need someone to teach you again the first principles of the oracles of God; and you have come to need milk and not solid food." (Hebrews 5:12)

"For this reason we must pay much closer attention to what we have heard, so that we do not drift away from it." (Hebrews 2:1)

"So faith comes from hearing, and hearing through the word of Christ." (Romans 10:17)

Controlled Speech

Commonly known in Christianese as "taming the tongue," the practice of being disciplined with what we say is another precursor to experiencing the mind of Christ. God brought all things into creation by his words. We are created in his image and, likewise, our words have power that we've yet to fully recognize.

"By faith we understand that the worlds were framed by the word of God, so that the things which are seen were not made of things which are visible." (Hebrews 11:3)

"By the word of the Lord the heavens were made, and all the host of them by the breath of His mouth." (Psalm 33:6)

Jesus even spoke of the power of the words we speak and our accountability for what we say.

"...if you have faith as a mustard seed, you will say to this mountain, 'Move from here to there,' and it will move; and nothing will be impossible for you." (Matthew 17:20)

"So the Lord said, 'If you have faith as a mustard seed, you can say to this mulberry tree, 'Be pulled up by the roots and be planted in the sea', and it would obey you." (Luke 17:6)

"But I tell you that men will have to give account on the day of judgment for every careless word they have spoken. For by your words you will be acquitted, and by your words you will be condemned." (Matthew 12:36-37)

When I recognized the seriousness of taking control of my words, I realized I needed to be quiet more often than I spoke and found these scriptures:

"In the multitudes of words sin is not lacking, but he who restrains his lips is wise." (Proverbs 10:19)

"Whoever guards his mouth and tongue keeps his soul from troubles." (Proverbs 21:23)

"Do not be rash with your mouth and let not your heart utter anything hastily before God. For God is in heaven, and you on earth; Therefore let your words be few." (Ecclesiastes 5:2)

"Avoid godless chatter, because those who indulge in it will become more and more ungodly." (2 Timothy 2:16 NIV)

So the words we speak will either be a creative force of life or a destructive force of death. They will have a positive impact or negative impact to an extent that we've yet to comprehend.

"The tongue can bring death or life; those who love to talk will reap the consequences." (Proverbs 18:21 NLT)

Facing the truth that we bless or curse by the words we speak places a great responsibility on us to take control of what we say. All that venture towards speaking only words that are positive and life giving find out that it takes a large amount of self-control. The scriptures frequently urge us to be attentive to our communication.

"Let no corrupting talk come out of your mouths, but only such as is good for building up, as fits the occasion, that it may give grace to those who hear." (Ephesians 4:29 ESV)

"Let your speech always be gracious, seasoned with salt, so that you may know how you ought to answer each person." (Colossians 4:6 ESV)

"Whoever desires to love life and see good days, let him keep his tongue from evil and his lips from speaking deceit." (1 Peter 3:10)

"There is one whose rash words are like sword thrusts, but the tongue of the wise brings healing." (Proverbs 12:18)

"A gentle tongue is a tree of life, but perverseness in it breaks the spirit." (Proverbs 15:4)

"My lips shall greatly rejoice when I sing to You, and my soul which You have redeemed. My tongue shall also talk of Your righteousness all day long." (Psalm 71:23-24)

We all stumble in many ways. Anyone who is never at fault in what they say is perfect, able to keep their whole body in check. When we put bits into the mouths of horses to make them obey us, we can turn the whole animal. Or take ships as an example. Although they are so large and are driven by strong winds, they are steered by a very small rudder wherever the pilot wants to go. Likewise, the tongue is a small part of the body, but it makes great boasts. Consider what a great forest is set on fire by a small spark. The tongue also is a fire, a world of evil among the parts of the body. It corrupts the whole body, sets the whole course of one's life on fire, and is itself set on fire by hell.

James 3:2-6

With the tongue we praise our Lord and Father, and with it we curse human beings, who have been made in God's likeness. Out of the same mouth come praise and cursing. My brothers and sisters, this should not be. Can both fresh water and salt water flow from the same spring?

James 3:9-11

"If anyone speaks, let him speak as the oracles of God. If anyone ministers, let him do it as with the ability which God supplies, that in all things God may be glorified through Jesus Christ, to whom belong the glory and dominion forever and ever, Amen." (1 Peter 4:11)

Jesus was known for speaking gracious words, meaning courteous, compassionate, and kind.

"And all spoke well of him and marveled at the gracious words that were coming from his mouth. And they said, 'Is not this Joseph's son?'" (Luke 4:22 ESV)

Cultivated Humility

I have used the word cultivate because it means "to foster the growth of" and if there is a quality that needs a great deal of fostering, it is humility.

Before falling from heaven to earth and turning into Satan, the original sin of the arch angel Lucifer was pride. In Isaiah 14:12-18, we're told about Lucifer considering himself so great that five times in this passage he said "I will" referring to exalting himself

above God.   Later, when Adam and Eve lived in the garden of
Eden, Satan tempted Eve to eat the forbidden fruit through pride.
Satan told Eve, "For God knows that in the day you eat of it your
eyes will be opened, and you will be like God, knowing good
and evil." (Genesis 3:5) He proposed that she would be like God
himself if she ate of the fruit.

Because of this, pride is at the very core of our sinful nature and
it is the opposite of humility. We can be prideful about anything.
Our homes, our belongings, our station in life, or our authority
among people and much more.

I appreciate what Benjamin Franklin said about it:

> In reality, there is, perhaps, no one of our natural passions
> so hard to subdue as pride. Disguise it, struggle with it, beat
> it down, stifle it, mortify it as much as one pleases, it is still
> alive, and will every now and then peep out and show itself;
> you will see it, perhaps, often in this history; for, even if I
> could conceive that I had completely overcome it, I should
> probably be proud of my humility.

The purity of heart displayed by Christ is reflected in his depth of
humility, and the Holy Spirit will reveal its substance to us as we
pursue the mind of Christ.

> Let this mind be in you which was also in Christ Jesus, who,
> being in the form of God, did not consider it robbery to be
> equal with God, but made Himself of no reputation, taking
> the form of a bondservant, and coming in the likeness of
> men. And being found in appearance as a man, He humbled
> Himself and became obedient to the point of death, even the
> death of the cross.

Philippians 2:5-8

The profoundness of this passage is hard to grasp upon simply reading it over and over. Meditate on the idea and consider that the Son of God came and relinquished his deity, his omnipotence (all powerful), omniscience (all knowing), and omnipresence (present everywhere). Just the thought of exchanging all that to become like mortal man takes my breath away. He lowered himself to become the unthinkable: mankind, who God himself had created. He learned to submit to God in all circumstances and became a catalyst of the unconditional love of God. Mankind had never seen such an expression of love, kindness, mercy, and grace. Nor had they heard truth and wisdom greater than that of King Solomon until Christ spoke.

He humbled himself and became a servant to all mankind. Not only that, but he became obedient to God to the point of death and even the death of the cross. Death on a cross was the most painful and humiliating death of that era, shaming the condemned in the worst way possible. It wasn't enough that Christ would have to die to redeem mankind but he had to be humiliated by crucifixion for sins he did not commit. Yet all of this was necessary to save man from the condemnation he deserved for his sins.

However, this was not the only reason Christ came to earth but was a necessary part of God's ultimate goal. We were created in the image of God (Gen. 1:26) and God is love (1 John 4:8). Adam and Eve were creatures created as God's love. Once they disobeyed, they were separated from God's love and became creatures of a cursed earth and blood was required for the forgiveness of men's sins. The blood of animals was shed in proxy of mankind (Lev. 17:11, Heb. 9:22).

The immeasurable love of God for mankind culminated in God the Father sacrificing his only Son for the complete and final remission of their sins so they could be restored to the family of God as beings of love. Remember, Christ endured the cross for the joy set before him (Heb. 12:2). Through his sacrifice, we have been restored to the family of God, enveloped by God's unconditional love, experiencing unwavering acceptance and benefits of being God's child.

"Let this mind be in you which was also in Christ Jesus," exhorts us to humble ourselves by serving others, abandoning our reputation and our need to be respected by others, becoming obedient to God alone. We have been saved to become the love of God to a lost and dying world. This is completely opposite to the carnal system that surrounds us- the pursuit of self-fulfillment and personal gratification.

In giving our lives over to God, our experiences are now meant for his purposes and not our own. Believers spend far too much time being concerned about what others think about them. Being humble eliminates the need for man's approval, but it is a thought battle that all who choose to grow into Christlikeness will encounter.

We no longer belong to ourselves. As Oswald Chambers once said, "If you are going to be used by God, he will take you through a multitude of experiences that are not meant for you at all. They are meant to make you useful in His hands."

"Or do you not know that your body is the temple of the Holy Spirit who is in you, whom you have from God, and you are not your own? For you were bought at a price; therefore glorify God in your body and in your spirit, which are God's." (1 Corinthians 6:19-20)

The quantum shift from a life of self-reliance to total reliance on God, complete trust in his fatherhood, and being an expression of his love to the world is entirely possible. Where self-reliance is considered by the world as being responsible with one's life, complete reliance on God is seen as foolishness at best.

Let no one deceive himself. If anyone among you thinks that he is wise in this age, let him become a fool that he may become wise. For the wisdom of this world is folly with God. For it is written, 'He catches the wise in their craftiness,' and again, 'The Lord knows the thoughts of the wise, that they are futile.'

1 Corinthians 3:18-20 (ESV)

This shift is only possible by living with the awareness of God's Spirit within us as our helper.

"But the Helper, the Holy Spirit, whom the Father will send in my name, he will teach you all things and bring to your remembrance all that I have said to you." John 14:26 (ESV) (see Acts 1: 5-8).

Finally, we need to understand that humility is the foundation which all spiritual virtues rest upon. What we know as the "fruit" of the Holy Spirit are godly virtues.

"But the fruit of the Spirit is love, joy, peace, longsuffering, kindness, goodness, faithfulness, gentleness, self-control. Against such there is no law." (Galatians 5:22-23 NKJV) ('No law' here simply means without any limit to them.)

Consider the fact that any one of these virtues will not be good "fruit" without flowing from a heart of humility. It is easy to be prideful, or take credit for when we show kindness or love. When we manage to have self-control, we may want to pat ourselves on the back. Humility *knows* that all this fruit comes from God's Holy Spirit and not our human efforts. All that is good and holy and just comes from God alone and he knows what is best for us.

Saint Augustine once said, "Humility is the foundation of all the other virtues hence, in the soul in which this virtue does not exist, there cannot be any other virtue except in mere appearance."

"For my thoughts are not your thoughts, neither are your ways my ways, declares the Lord." (Isaiah 55:8 NIV)

When we become aware of how limited our knowledge is, it establishes a basis for humility. Once again, the world's system prides itself on being knowledgeable. The reasoning of the intellect is a human downfall that feeds the pride of man. We easily fall into the trap of pride and must learn to judge every thought accordingly.

"For I say, through the grace given to me, to everyone who is among you, not to think of himself more highly than he ought to think, but to think soberly, as God has dealt to each one a measure of faith." (Romans 12:3 NKJV)

"True humility is not thinking less of yourself; it is thinking of yourself less." C.S. Lewis

Consistent Obedience

As you may recall, Jesus was aware of what he had to endure to secure our salvation but asked his Father if he would change the plan to avoid the shame and extreme pain of the crucifixion, but mostly having his Father forsake him. He had never been separated from God the Father!

> Father, if it is Your will, take this cup away from Me; nevertheless not My will, but Yours, be done. Then an angel appeared to Him from heaven, strengthening Him. And being in agony, He prayed more earnestly. Then His sweat became like great drops of blood falling down to the ground.
>
> Luke 22:42-44

This example of Christ is unfathomable. How could we ever rise to such a level of obedience to God, obeying him no matter what he asks of us? It is only possible if we develop a deeply personal relationship and learn to live in his presence. Only as we make room for a full relationship with God is obedience possible. Jesus made it possible for us to experience full obedience by his very own complete obedience. He traded his obedience for our disobedience.

> But don't just listen to God's word. You must do what it says. Otherwise, you are only fooling yourselves. For if you listen to the word and don't obey, it is like glancing at your face in a mirror. You see yourself, walk away, and forget what you look like. But if you look carefully into the perfect law that sets you free, and if you do what it says and don't forget what you heard, then God will bless you for doing it.

> James 1:22–25 (NLT)

"Because we have these promises, dear friends, let us cleanse ourselves from everything that can defile our body or spirit. And let us work toward complete holiness because we fear God." (2 Corinthians 7:1 NLT)

Notice that it says to "work toward" complete holiness. It is a process. In pursuing obedience, we begin with baby steps by obeying the mandate to put away deeds of darkness. (Col. 3: 5-10, Eph. 4: 22-24, 1 Pet. 1:14, Titus 2: 12-13, 1 Thess. 4:3, Eph. 4:31.)

As we begin to mature, we address the items listed above: how we hear, what we speak, and how to cultivate humility through servanthood. From there, we become familiar with God's voice instructing us and obey his directives.

It is not unusual for God to ask you to do something that other believers will not understand. The scriptures are full of such examples such as Abraham being told to sacrifice his son who was his heir of promise in Genesis 22, or Noah being told to build an ark in a world without rain (Genesis 6), or Paul being told by the prophet Agabus the suffering he would go through if he went to Jerusalem, facing arrest and persecution in Acts 21:10-13. But Paul was certain God wanted him to go there despite warnings of personal harm. We must all have a personal relationship not only with Jesus Christ, but with our heavenly Father who knows what our ultimate purpose is that will bring him glory. These are but a few examples of when people of faith were asked to do things that made no sense in human terms.

Because of this, the mature Christian will be faced with mandates that will cause friends, family, and even brethren to question their actions and even pass judgement on them. At this point of maturity, you aren't concerned what others think, but focused on obeying the instructions of the Lord.

"If they persecuted Me, they will also persecute you." (John 15:20)

"God is God. Because he is God, He is worthy of my trust and obedience. I will find rest nowhere but, in His holy will that is unspeakably beyond my largest notions of what he is up to." (Elisabeth Elliot)

Chapter Eight

Level Up

Clearly, to approach putting on the mind of Christ, we must grow up. There are different levels of growth in Christ. For every new level of growth, there is a new demonic strategy to keep you from growing into Christlikeness. By this I mean that what Satan would use against a new Christian is useless against a more mature Christian. The more our heart yearns for God's heart, the more tailored attack will be devised to thwart one's growth into the mind of Christ. I want to also say that when you enter a new level, angels are assigned to you and the Holy Spirit within you will always assist you. You are never alone in this battle. As a matter of fact, Christ has already overcome the enemy, so Satan is just trying to deceive us with his lies (Colossians 2:15).

There are some Christians that enter the faith and get comfortable in their change of direction in life, remaining there without moving further into intimacy with God. Others jump into their new life with a zeal and relentless fervor to know everything Christ died for us to experience. Some have such a transformative experience with Jesus that they are pushed directly into maturity by God himself. How great would that be? But for a large number of us, we are on a path of choosing how and when we go deeper in our relationship with God as we have a free will. Even though the Holy Spirit will prompt us to grow in our faith, we make the final decision.

The scriptures speak of our choices in terms of a narrow gate and a wide gate.

"Enter through the narrow gate. For wide is the gate and broad is the road that leads to destruction, and many enter through it. But small is the gate and narrow the road that leads to life, and only a few find it." (Matthew 7:13-14 NIV)

Most commentaries believe that the broad road leads to hell due to the word "destruction," but my studies have convinced me that the broad way leads to a destruction of God's intention for our lives and many Christians choose the broad way that requires little self-sacrifice. It's quite sobering that Jesus is saying that few find the narrow road to true life.

Beyond this, the New Testament Greek speaks about the different levels of growth in Christ. I learned about this from Dr. Richard Ledet, Pastor and President of Time for Revival Teaching Ministry. Most people don't know him. I have been immensely blessed to know him on a personal level for the better part of my life. He is humble, yet brilliant and has researched extensively the progression of Christian growth as reflected within scripture. Dr. Ledet has identified the five stages of Christian development according to the Greek language used in the New Testament. This helps us to consider if we are moving forward in Christ or have become stagnant.

"Examine yourselves as to whether you are in the faith. Test yourselves. Do you not know yourselves, that Christ Jesus is in you? - unless indeed you are disqualified. But I trust that you will know that we are not disqualified." (2 Corinthians 13:5-6)

Finally, Dr. Ledet's study is extensive. With his permission, I have condensed it to present the most meaningful scriptures for each stage of growth.

STAGE 1: NEPIOS

Strong's Concordance# 3516 "νήπιος [nepios /nay•pee•os/] adj. 1- an infant, little child. 2- a minor, not of age. 3- metaphorically used for childish, untaught, unskilled."

Paul addresses the *nepios* in 1 Corinthians 3: 1-3. "And I, Brethren, could not speak to you as spiritual people but as to carnal, as to *babes* in Christ. I fed you with milk and not solid food; for until now you were not able to receive it, and even now you are still not able; for you are still carnal."

He encourages the *nepios* in Ephesus to grow up in their faith in Ephesians 4:14-15, "that we should no longer be *children*, tossed to and fro and carried about with every wind of doctrine, by the trickery of men, in the cunning craftiness of deceitful plotting, but, speaking the truth in love, may grow up in all things into Him who is the head- Christ ..."

Hebrews 5 points out that some believers have been slack concerning their commitment to grow in their faith. Unfortunately, it's far too often that people become Christians, but simply integrate him into their lifestyle without trying to be transformed into Christ.

> For though by this time you ought to be teachers, you need someone to teach you again the first principles of the oracles of God; and you have come to need milk and not solid food. For everyone who partakes only of milk is unskilled in the word of righteousness, for he is a babe. But solid food belongs to those who are of full age, that is, those who by reason of use have their senses exercised to discern both good and evil.

> Hebrews 5:12-14

STAGE 2: PAIDION

The new Strong's dictionary of Hebrew and Greek words – #3813;

"παιδίον paidion, pahee-dee´-on." The term *paidion* was used for children after they were approximately two years old, up to the age of eleven or twelve (prior to their bar-mitzvah for boys).

In this stage, the believer gets to know their Heavenly Father and begins to develop a relationship with him . "I write to you, little *children*, because you have known the Father." (1 John 2:13) The Father doesn't seem so far away as with the *nepios*. The *paidion* faith grows to recognize the Father as the one who loves and cares for him.

This stage is marked by substantial growth in spiritual knowledge and understanding of the word of God. "So the *child* grew and became strong in spirit ..." (Luke 1:80) "And the Child grew and became strong in spirit, filled with wisdom; and the grace of God was upon Him." (Luke 2:40)

It is also at this stage that Christ used this word to show the traits of a believer.

"Assuredly, I say to you, unless you are converted and becomes as little *children*, you will by no means enter the kingdom of heaven. Therefore whoever humbles himself as this little child is the greatest in the kingdom of heaven." (Matthew 18:3-4)

Children during this stage are trusting, humble, carefree, loving, innocent, and responsive to God. We are to be converted and become as they are in this way during this second stage.

In the spiritual stage of the *paidion*, they also begin to learn about deception, and recognizing true doctrine as opposed to the false.

"Little *children*, it is the last hour; and as you have heard that the Antichrist is coming, even now many antichrists have come, by which we know that it is the last hour." (1 John 2:18)

STAGE 3: TEKNON

Enhanced Strong's Lexicon #G5043 "τέκνον [teknon /tek•non/] n. Used in an affectionate address, such as patrons, helpers, teachers and the like employ: my child. Used in the New Testament as pupils or disciples being called children of their teachers, because the latter by their instruction nourish the minds of their pupils and mold their characters."

It is used to identify those growing genuine in their faith, as Paul called his spiritual offspring.

"To Timothy, a beloved *son*." (2 Timothy 1:2)

"I appeal to you for my *son* Onesimus, who I have begotten while in my chains …" (Philemon 1:10)

During this stage it becomes more evident that they are a true disciple of Jesus Christ, growing in knowledge and understanding. The disciples seemed to be in this third stage of spiritual growth as Christ approached his crucifixion.

> Little *children*, I shall be with you a little while longer. You will seek Me; and as I said to the Jews, 'Where I am going you cannot come,' so now I say to you. A new command I give to you, that you love one another; as I have loved you, that you also love one another. By this all will know that you are My disciples, if you have love for one another.
>
> John 13:33-35

The apostle John used this term when addressing his disciples in 3 John 1:3-4. "For I rejoiced greatly when brethren came and testified of the truth that is in you, just as you walk in the truth. I have no greater joy than to hear that my *children* walk in the truth."

The *teknon* believer is coming into more maturity, having established a solid foundation in Christ.

"The Spirit Himself bears witness with our spirit that we are *children* of God." (Romans 8:16)

STAGE 4: HUIOS

Enhanced Strong's Lexicon – 5207 "υἱός [huios /hwee•os/] – Used for those who revere God as their father, the pious worshippers of God, those who in character and life resemble God, those who are governed by the Spirit of God."

This term was used predominantly of Jesus Christ, as enjoying the supreme love of God, united to him in affectionate intimacy, privy to his saving councils, obedient to the Father's will in all his acts. By the time Jesus was thirty years of age, he was in the *huios* stage.

> When He had been baptized, Jesus came up immediately from the water; and behold, the heavens were opened to Him, and He saw the Spirit of God descending like a dove and alighting upon Him. And suddenly a voice came from heaven, saying, 'This is my beloved *Son*, in whom I am well pleased.'
>
> Matthew 3:16-17

> He said to them, 'But who do you say that I am?' Simon Peter answered and said, 'You are the Christ, the *Son* of the living God.' Jesus answered and said to him, 'Blessed are you, Simon Bar-Jonah, for flesh and blood has not revealed this to you, but My Father who is in heaven.
>
> Matthew 16:15-17

In the first three stages of growth, the believer is learning to hear the voice of the Holy Spirit. By this fourth stage, they are well acquainted with his voice and promptly respond to his leading.

"For as many as are led by the Spirit of God, these are the *sons* of God." (Romans 8:14)

The *huios* is marked by spiritual maturity reflected in knowledge of the word of God, spiritual discernment, fruit of the Spirit, operation of their spiritual gifts, Christlikeness, and a reverence for the things of God. This is the stage where true church leaders arise.

"You are all *sons* of the light and sons of the day. We are not of the night, nor of the darkness." (1 Thessalonians 5:5)

STAGE 5: TELEIOS

Enhanced Strong's Lexicon #G5046 "τέλειος [teleios /tel•i•os/] adj. Used to indicate completion as in finished, perfect. Used as in not lacking anything necessary to completeness. Used to describe human integrity and virtue; full grown, adult, of full age, mature."

Bible commentaries consistently refer to the *teleios* as the man who has reached his goal, the man who is self-controlled. That being the case in speech, he is able also to bridle the whole body, because the tongue resists control more than any other area of behavior. The use of the word "bridle" reflects speaking with restrained guidance. The *teleios* stage is the goal, the purpose of our development. God desires all Christians to develop into this maturity. It is perfection within the constraints of flesh and blood, but the perfection here is becoming all that God desires us to be as we serve him on earth: walking as loving, obedient, and humble reflectors of his glory, Jesus Christ.

"I press toward the goal or the prize of the upward call of God in Christ Jesus. Therefore, let us, as many as are *mature*, have this mind; and if in anything you think otherwise, God will reveal even this to you." (Philippians 3:14-15)

"Therefore you shall be *perfect*, just as your Father in heaven is *perfect*." (Matthew 5:48)

"Jesus said to him, 'If you want to be *perfect*, go, sell what you have and give to the poor, and you will have treasure in heaven; and come, follow me.'" (Matthew 19:21)

"Epaphras, who is one of you, a bondservant of Christ, greets you, always laboring fervently for you in prayers, that you may stand *perfect* and complete in all the will of God." (Colossians 4:12)

The Christian in the *teleios* state is only concerned with growing others up into Christ. They live from a place of humility and servanthood, focused on training others in the word of God for the work of the ministry.

"...until we all come to the unity of the faith and of the knowledge of the Son of God, to a perfect man, to the measure of the stature of the fullness of Christ." (Ephesians 4:13)

"Him we preach, warning every man and teaching every man in all wisdom, that we may present every man *perfect* in Christ Jesus." (Colossians 1:28)

"When I was a child, I spoke as a child, I understood as a child, I thought as a child; but when I became a man, I put away childish things." (1 Corinthians 13:11)

I'm closing out this chapter with a passage of scripture for you to read and meditate on. Selah.

> Grace and peace be multiplied to you in the knowledge of God and of Jesus our lord, as His divine power has given to us all things that pertain to life and godliness, through the knowledge of Him who called us by glory and virtue, by which have been given to us exceedingly great and precious promises, that through these you may be partakers of the divine nature, having escaped the corruption that is in the world through lust.

> But also for this very reason, giving all diligence, add to your

faith virtue, to virtue knowledge, to knowledge self-control, to self-control perseverance, to perseverance godliness, to godliness brotherly kindness, and to brotherly kindness love. For if these things are yours and abound, you will be neither barren nor unfruitful in the knowledge of our Lord Jesus Christ.

For he who lacks these things is shortsighted, even to blindness, and forgotten that he was cleansed from his old sins. Therefore, brethren, be even more diligent to make your call and election sure, for if you do these things you will never stumble; for so an entrance will be supplied to you abundantly into the everlasting kingdom of our Lord and Savior Jesus Christ.

2 Peter 1:2-11

"Youth ends when egotism does; maturity begins when one lives for others." (Hermann Hesse)

Chapter Nine

Spiritual Rest

It seems to take a long time to mature into spiritual rest, but I want to exhort you to approach life from the position of resting in God. In accepting the work of Christ on the cross, laboring for God's acceptance is over. He paid the price for us to have complete forgiveness from past, present, and future sins by his eternal sacrifice. We are forever accepted by God and don't have to seek his approval any longer since we have already received it through Jesus Christ.

The rest provided by Christ is radical. For one thing, you don't rest from physical labor, but are in a mental posture of rest while you work. If we are still stressed out while working, we have yet to enter the full provision spiritual rest provides.

It helps to look at how Christ lived from a position of this rest, knowing that his Father had everything prepared for his purpose on earth. We have yet to grasp the importance of entering the same rest.

If we would live from a place of believing God has everything prepared for us, we would live in peace.

> For by grace you have been saved through faith, and that not of yourselves; it is the gift of God, not of works, lest anyone

should boast. For we are his workmanship, created in Christ Jesus for good works, which God prepared beforehand that we should walk in them.

Ephesians 2:8-10

As with Christ, our heavenly Father has already prepared a course for our lives and desires that we walk according to his purpose for us. Not a detail is missed as he knows exactly what we need to be conformed to the image of his Son and fulfill our destiny in God's Kingdom.

"And we know that for those who love God all things work together for good, for those who are called according to his purpose." (Romans 8:28)

"For I know the plans I have for you, declares the Lord, plans for welfare and not for evil, to give you a future and a hope." (Jeremiah 29:11)

"In him we have obtained an inheritance, having been predestined according to the purpose of him who works all things according to the counsel of his will..." (Ephesians 1:11)

As conveyed in earlier chapters, being God's child doesn't mean life will be easy. In fact, Jesus said, "These things I have spoken to you, that in Me you may have peace. In the world you will have tribulation; but be of good cheer, I have overcome the world." (John 16:33) He didn't say "might," but "you will."

Tribulation comes to us in a variety of ways, but even on a simple level, life's challenges should be tempered by the peace of God within us. For example, take any day you've experienced in which nothing seemed to go well: your computer is problematic, you get a flat tire running errands or on your way to work, and you spill your lunch on your white shirt before going to a meeting. We all have such days in life. How do we respond to such events? Are we angry, frustrated, anxious, fearful, or spewing out obscenities? Do we take such frustrations out on our loved ones or those we come in contact with throughout the day? If so, we are yet carnal.

> For though by this time you ought to be teachers, you need someone to teach you again the first principles of the oracles of God; and you have come to need milk and not solid food. For everyone who partakes only of milk is unskilled in the word of righteousness, for he is a babe. But solid food belongs to those who are of full age, that is, those who by reason of use have their senses exercised to discern both good and evil.
>
> Hebrews 5:12-13

The "first principles" are basic truths, foundational to all spiritual development. Being "unskilled in the word of righteousness" doesn't mean one lacks the information about our righteousness of God in Christ, but they are unskilled because they have not focused on such truths in order to practice them in all of life's circumstances. The "solid food" is to be consumed by those who have given full attention to the basic truths of the faith and are of full age (matured by thought and practice) to the point of being able to digest it, or "stomach it."

> Therefore, leaving the discussion of the elementary principles of Christ, let us go on to perfection, not laying again the foundation of repentance from dead works and of faith toward God, of the doctrine of baptisms, of laying on of hands, of resurrection of the dead, and of eternal judgment. And this we will do if God permits.
>
> Hebrews 6:1-3

It is time we move on to what Christ has called us for. Every experience is an opportunity to grow spiritually by changing our thoughts and reactions to them. We can take deep breaths and thank God that he will work all things out, devote our hearts to him, and enter the sphere of worship which *always* makes things better. Although demons may taunt us through circumstantial challenges, everything can be used to grow us up into Christ.

As we repeatedly practice recognizing God is working all things for our spiritual development and to our best advantage, the stress and emotional pain of our carnal mind will be replaced with the peace that passes understanding. Such peace carries with it a rest for the soul.

"And the peace of God, which surpasses all understanding, will guard your hearts and minds through Christ Jesus." (Philippians 4:7)

God's desire is for us to recognize that all things we experience are meant to further our relationship with him. The element of trust is critical to gaining the most from each and every circumstance in our lives. His desire is to bless us with all spiritual blessings (Ephesians 1:3).

"There remains therefore a rest for the people of God. For he who has entered His rest has himself also ceased from his works as God did from His. Let us therefore be diligent to enter that rest..." (Hebrews 4:9-11a)

Remember that God did not rest on the seventh day of creation because he was tired. He rested because the work was complete. In the same way Christ has completed the work for us. We only have to walk in our destiny, fully trusting in him . Living with a complete trust in the promises of God and that he has moved us into a divine plan, will help us, care for us, provide for us, and clear the path as we pursue growing into being Christlike. Rest can be experienced every moment of our lives as we trust in what Christ has accomplished for us. We have nothing to prove, nothing to protect and nothing to fear. This is truly good news.

"Come to me all you who labor and are heavy laden and I will give you rest. Take my yoke upon you and learn from Me, for I am gentle and lowly in heart, and you will find rest for your souls. For My yoke is easy and My burden is light." (Matthew 11: 28-30)

The key words here are "learn from me" since we need to learn how to enter his rest. Part of what Christ endured on our behalf was so that we would not have to struggle, strive, worry, or care about what life brings our way. We have a total assurance that our Heavenly Father is working all things out for our benefit and for his good pleasure in our lives.

"And we know that all things work together for good to those who love God, to those who are the called according to His purpose." (Romans 8:28)

A prime example of this is that the Apostle Paul taught believers about being free while being himself in chains in a Roman prison. Just read the book of Romans with Paul's chains in mind and you'll understand. Paul lived from a position of rest in not only the accomplished work of Christ, but trusting that no matter what he went through, God was with him and would be glorified through it. He trusted God in all things, which led him to a place of peace amidst intolerable hardship.

> And see, now I go bound in the spirit to Jerusalem, not knowing the things that will happen to me there, except that the Holy Spirit testifies in every city, saying that chains and tribulations await me. But none of these things move me; nor do I count my life dear to myself, so that I may finish my race with joy, and the ministry which I received from the Lord Jesus, to testify to the gospel of the grace of God.
>
> Acts 20:22-24

"Love turns work into rest." (Teresa of Ávila)

Chapter Ten

A Consuming Fire

It's a wonderful feeling to be free from old patterns of thought and certainly worth all the effort. The carnal clutter in our mind has been like a wet blanket on the fire of God within us. Any believer can recall the passion and zeal that comes with encountering Christ. As John the Baptist said, "He will baptize you with the Holy Spirit and with fire," (Matthew 3:11) and that fire is the presence of the Holy Spirit remaining within us. I don't want the fire within me to be a pilot light, waiting to be lit. I want it to be constantly aflame with love for both God and others.

We are the ones who keep that fire burning bright as we keep our life focused on becoming Christlike. Our hearts are to crave the word of God, desire to pray in everything we do, and desire to be with other believers. If such things seem more like a burden to us, then we have forsaken our personal relationship with God and replaced it with religious activities.

"For this reason I remind you to fan into flame the gift of God, which is in you through the laying on of my hands." (2 Timothy 1:6 ESV)

The flame is from God and it is within you. It is fanned as we connect with God on an intimate level. Spiritual activities that have become a religious practice to us don't have fire in them. It's when our aim is to encounter God that the fire within us grows. God is a consuming fire that conjoins our flame as we connect (Hebrews 12:29).

Saint Augustine said, "God loves each of us as if there were only one of us." It is very hard to comprehend that Almighty God wants to meet with me, that his passion burns for me and that he sacrificed his only Son because of his desire that I know him. This fiery passion God has for each of us is mystifying to our limited understanding.

However, if you've known the Lord for some time, you can recall times that you unmistakably encountered God in prayer, worship, or in his word. Jesus pointed this out as the goal in his incredible prayer in John 17:3, "And this is eternal life, that *they may know You*, the only true God, and Jesus Christ whom You have sent." God wants us each to know him in a very tangible way.

Our fire grows brighter through meditation

Quieting ourselves in his presence is a holy place to commune with our heavenly Father. As he told Israel through the prophet Isaiah, "In quietness and confidence will be your strength," (Isaiah 60:15). The "confidence" mentioned here has to do with our recognition of God's desire for us to talk with him and be confident of his immeasurable love for us. Christ reconciled us to the Father and he wants us to be confident that we can approach him and are accepted by him .

Repeatedly giving thought to God's word, his faithfulness, and his presence in our lives will create positive neural pathways in our brains.

"Make me understand the way of Your precepts; so shall I meditate on Your wonderful works." (Psalm 119:27)

"My eyes are awake through the night watches, that I may meditate on Your word." (Psalm 119:148)

"When I remember You on my bed, I meditate on You in the night watches." (Psalm 63:6)

"May my meditation be sweet to Him; I will be glad in the Lord." (Psalm 104:34)

"I have more understanding than all my teachers, for your testimonies are my meditations." (Psalm 119:99)

"For they (God's words) are life to those who find them, and health to all their flesh." (Proverbs 4:22)

"This Book of the Law shall not depart from your mouth, but you shall meditate on it day and night, that you may observe to do according to all that is written in it. For then you will make your way prosperous and then you will have good success." (Joshua 1:8)

In this passage from the book of Joshua, we're told that if we meditate on God's Word, our way will be prosperous and we will have success. I also like how Proverbs 4:22 tells us that meditating on God's Word will bring health to all our flesh. There's so much in the Word of God that will strengthen our faith, our physical body, and our entire lives.

Our fire grows brighter through reading the Bible

There are many ways to read the word of God. By that I mean, there are plans available to read the Bible in a year or read the Bible by themes like hope, prayer, faithfulness, friendships, the Holy Spirit, etc. These are all a blessing. Yet most importantly is that we read the word of God with faith that God will speak to us personally. It's not to be read as a self-help book. It's to be read as a love letter to each of us. In other words, you can't have my relationship with Jesus. You must have your own. Simply going to church or a home group is not enough. He wants you to know him.

> None of them shall teach his neighbor, and none his brother, saying 'Know the Lord,' *for all shall know Me, from the least of them to the greatest of them.* For I will be merciful to their unrighteousness, and their sins and their lawless deeds I will remember no more.

Hebrews 8:11-12

When we approach the word of God on a personal level, it changes us. So many times I have had scriptures that I have studied over the years come into my mind to help me through life's challenges, as well as help those that God has connected me to. There is nothing like the power of God's word. We need to read it with faith in its power to change us and renew our minds.

Again, Christ overcame Satan in the desert by speaking the word of God, saying "It is written." Each of us should know the word of God well enough to use it as a sword against the enemy.

"I have stored up your word in my heart, that I might not sin against you." (Psalm 119:11 ESV)

"The law of his God is in his heart; his steps do not slip." (Psalm 37:31 ESV)

In times of meditation, we can refer to the following scriptures that tell us what to think about.

> Finally, brethren, whatever things are true, whatever things are noble, whatever things are just, whatever things are pure, whatever things are lovely, whatever things are of good report, if there be any virtue and if there is anything praiseworthy – meditate on these things.

Philippians 4:8

"Set your mind on things above, not on things on the earth."
(Colossians 3:2)

"For those who live according to the flesh set their minds on the
things of the flesh, but those who live according to the Spirit, the
things of the Spirit." (Romans 8:5)

"...speaking to one another in psalms, hymns, and spiritual songs,
singing and making melody in your heart to the Lord, giving
thanks always for all things to God the Father in the name of our
Lord Jesus Christ..." (Ephesians 5:19-20)

Our fire grows brighter as we actively trust him

Learning to surrender all our concerns to God requires an
unwavering trust of his word, his love for us, and his promises to
us. Since Satan tempted Eve to mistrust what God said about the
tree, we have a natural bent towards doubting God. Add to that
the fact that we haven't seen him and you realize it's a flat-out
miracle that we believe in God at all.

Our Adamic nature always has us scrambling for safety and
security, with an insatiable appetite for worldly things. In Christ,
we have received complete safety, everlasting security and a new
desire for the things of God's Kingdom. As a matter of fact, Jesus
told us that the Father knows what we need before we ask him
(Matthew 6:8).

As we resist our natural inclination to strive on our own and
actively seek to trust God with everything in our lives, we gain
a peace that the world cannot offer. This peace provides rest for
our souls in the midst of whatever difficulties we are experiencing.
People can't understand how we can have peace in the worst of
circumstances. It is experienced as we trust God no matter what
we are going through, knowing he is working all things for our
good (Romans 8:28). People typically think of peace as a time in

which we have no concerns, however this is a peace in the midst of life's storms, a steadiness and sureness that comes from God alone. It was this peace that allowed Jesus to remain asleep in the boat during a violent storm.

> Now when He got into the boat, His disciples followed Him. And suddenly a great tempest arose on the sea, so that the boat was covered with the waves. But He was asleep. Then His disciples came to Him and awoke Him saying, 'Lord save us! We are perishing!' But He said to them, 'Why are you fearful, O you of little faith?' Then He arose and rebuked the winds and the sea, and there was a great calm. So the men marveled, saying, 'Who can this be, that even the winds and the sea obey Him?'

> Matthew 8: 23-27

"Be anxious for nothing, but in everything by prayer and supplication, with thanksgiving, let your requests be made known to God; and the peace of God, which surpasses all understanding, will guard your hearts and minds through Christ Jesus." (Philippians 4: 6-7)

The more we refuse to be concerned with every day challenges and actively seek to trust him, the more we experience his deep love for us. Get to know him.

Our fire grows brighter as we worship him

The place of worship is a most sacred place when it is from a heart of love for God. It is one thing to participate in corporate worship. It is quite another to worship God when you are alone. Transformation is cultivated when we worship him in solitude. I guarantee that you will sense his presence for quite some time afterwards. "God inhabits the praises of his people" (Psalm 22:3) will be experienced without a doubt.

Give some thought to Zephaniah 3:17, "The Lord your God is in your midst, The Mighty One, will save; He will rejoice over you with gladness, He will quiet you with His love, He will rejoice over you with singing."

How can we not respond with adoration? What could be more important in life than knowing this loving God, the maker of all things? So easily do the things of this world distract us with trivial matters.

"God is our refuge and strength, a very present help in trouble." (Psalm 46:1 KJV)

My friends, we were created for so much more. Let's just go for it while we still have time.

"Aim at heaven and you will get earth thrown in. Aim at earth and you get neither." (C.S. Lewis)

Chapter Eleven

Know Love

"Now hope does not disappoint, because the love of God has been poured out in our by the hearts by the Holy Spirit who was given to us." (Romans 5:5)

At this point it's important for us to talk about love. Now that we understand that being born again makes us a new creation designed in love (i.e. the image of God) we need to consider the difference between worldly conditional love and Gods unconditional love. They are vastly disparate.

We don't know love because the love passed down through generations of fallen man is twisted. As a species that has been seeking fulfillment through others, we have been in a tumultuous identity crisis basing our identity on our needs and how people respond to them. For instance, when we are kind, generous, and loving to people, if they don't reciprocate we judge them and feel "hurt." That was never the case with Christ. He demonstrated God's love and gets crucified for it! If anyone had a reason to feel "hurt," it was Jesus. Instead, on the cross he said, "Father forgive them, for they do not know what they do." (Luke 23:34) If we yield to being vessels of God's love, then we will love others without any expectation of a return. We love because he first loved us and love people because he loves them.

To love others as God loves them seems insurmountable, but it isn't. Christ came to demonstrate God's love and he did so in human form, proving that in him we are capable of living as vessels of love on earth. It is disheartening to acknowledge how inept we are at loving as Christ did. Fortunately, God gave us a chapter to teach us about his love.

Written by the Apostle Paul, 1 Corinthians 13 is known as the love chapter of the New Testament. It is read at weddings, anniversaries, and has even been set to music. We hear it or read it, but most of us have yet to comprehend the severity of its words. The love of this passage is godly and looks nothing like the love we experience from the world. Since the love of the world is self-serving, based on personal feelings, humans treat others differently if personal needs aren't met. Such love takes offense, rejects others, and at times will seek revenge for perceived wrongdoing, even to the point of murder. It always seeks its own pleasure and satisfaction. Even in doing things for others, carnal love is merely serving its desire for self-satisfaction and self-gain.

"My people come to you, as they usually do, and sit before you to hear your words, but they do not put them into practice. Their mouths speak of love, but their hearts are greedy for unjust gain." (Ezekiel 33:31 NIV)

Because of this, it is infinitely important that we confront what is not godly love in our lives by examining this text. Personally, I revisit this text often and use it as a barometer to make sure I'm remaining in his love and repent for where I'm failing to do so.

The first three verses are establishing the fact that love is more important than any spiritual gifting and that any actions devoid of love have no eternal value. It is the intent of verses four through seven to excise our heart of stone by the sword of the Spirit and replace it with a heart of flesh that is alive in God's love.

Love is patient, love is kind. It does not envy, it does not boast, it is not proud. It does not dishonor others, it is not self-seeking, it is not provoked, it keeps no record of wrongs. Love does not delight in evil but rejoices with the truth. It always protects, always trusts, always hopes, always perseveres.

1 Corinthians 13:4-7 NIV

It's important to recognize that each of the qualities apply in *all* situations. Not just in relationships, but in all areas of our lives because we've been restored to God's love. I encourage you to take the time to meditate on the concepts as we consider them.

Love is patient: Patience directly relates to waiting and in this technological era, people have grown accustomed to getting what they want *now*. The frustration of having to wait spills over into all of life. There are many reasons that people grow impatient, yet the core of it all is self-centeredness. We want things done according to our timeline and rarely take into consideration what others have to do or what they are having to deal with themselves. As Christians, we can even get impatient with God, waiting for him to do something in our lives. Pretty sad when you think about it. When we learn to love as a new creation, we realize every person is of value to God and that we need to consider others before ourselves. Think about your level of impatience.

Love is kind: Particularly in America, people are too busy to take the time to show kindness. Essentially, mankind is obsessed with their own lives. People can be unkind or mean which usually flows from feeling inadequate or believing their self-esteem is being threatened. Even when people go through a painful experience, it's common to lash out at others as a coping mechanism. If you've never been prone to being kind to others, it helps to start out the day with a prayer for opportunities to show kindness to others. It's amazing how different a day can be with such prayers.

It does not envy: Envy is a tragic experience since it's all about comparing oneself to others. It can be about possessions, appearance, someone's station in life, their spouse, their children, and so on. It feeds off of a person's poor self- image, lack of self-worth, and a victim mentality. Some people even consider being envied as evidence that they're successful in life. Envy also evokes strong feelings at times, but at the very least it is a subtle thought about another person. If we understand how important we are to God, we will be content with who we are and what we have.

"Keep your lives free from the love of money and be content with what you have, because God has said, 'Never will I leave you; never will I forsake you.'" (Hebrews 13:5)

Any thoughts or feelings that compare you to others are from the old Adamic nature. Give attention to destroying such thoughts and replace them with thoughts of God's deep love for you.

It does not boast: People boast because they want others to think well of them, basically due to insecurities about their value. In essence, the person who is boasting has engaged in self-praise, an act of human autonomy without acknowledgment of God. More importantly, boasting is the opposite of humility which is the foundational trait of Christlikeness.

"But God forbid that I should boast except in the cross of our Lord Jesus Christ, by whom the world has been crucified to me, and I to the world." (Galatians 6:14) What an amazing scripture this is.

It is not proud: One of the most profound acts of Jesus Christ was at the Passover dinner where he washed the feet of his disciples (John 13: 1-17). This is the antithesis of pride. In fallen humanity, we easily love those who look up to us, but such love is bereft of humility, seeking self-fulfillment and self-gratification. May we always examine our actions and measure them against the Spirit of

Christ that washes another's feet.

It does not dishonor others: I find this an interesting use of words. We dishonor others by bringing shame upon them through gossip or judgment of their actions. We dishonor others when we are disrespectful or treat them in a demeaning manner. Honoring others is believing in Christ in them to see them through their trials, respecting their personal relationship with the Lord and remaining non-judgmental. There is no way we can understand everyone's personal journey with the Lord because it's just that: personal. In fact, our Father is so personal that he will give us a new name that will only be known by him and us (Revelation 2:17). We need to show honor to others that are so beloved of God, respecting their individuality regardless of their station in life, societal status, or spiritual position. When we see them struggling in life, we who are strong are to strengthen them, not judge them.

"We who are strong have an obligation to bear with the failings of the weak, and not to please ourselves. Let each of us please his neighbor for his good, to build him up." (Romans 15:1-2 (ESV)

It is not self-seeking: Paul is having to deal with the carnality and chaos in the church at Corinth, all borne of self-seeking which is the direct opposite of love. If you read all of First Corinthians, you'll see that Paul is confronting their attitudes that are against love (divisive, judgmental, legal disputes, dishonoring communion, and preferential treatment of spiritual gifts). But the love of God seeks what is in the best interest of others. The Greek reading of the phrase "is not self-seeking" literally means "does not seek the things of self." The ESV version reads "does not insist on its own way" which certainly cuts to the core of the matter. If we are demanding our own way, claiming our rights over the rights of others, and insisting on being noticed, we are not walking in love. As the disciples were seeking a place of recognition in God's Kingdom, Jesus made it obvious that their thinking was faulty.

"...whoever desires to become great among you shall be your servant. And whoever of you desires to be first shall be slave to all. For even the Son of Man did not come to be served, but to serve, and to give His life a ransom for many." (Mark 10:43-45)

Is not provoked: Some versions read "is not easily angered" but anger conjures up very specific reactions, where the word provoke provides us with a much broader perspective. It has to do with evoking or inciting an emotion or reaction to what is taking place. Godly love is not reactionary. It doesn't have any "buttons" that can be pushed, is not touchy and certainly is not hostile toward others. There is an element of peace with God's love that, when embraced, places us in an attitude of complete love for others with no personal feelings to defend. Within this love, people can't hurt us since we have died to our old sinful self that was touchy-feely at the least. Everyone knows what it feels like to have an emotional "button" pushed. We need to give attention to what irks or provokes us and examine why we are so vulnerable to such things.

It keeps no record of wrongs: What a gift that God no longer remembers our sins and wrongdoings (Hebrews 8:12). Because of our sinful nature, it is difficult for us to forget the former wrongdoings of others. The brain actually marks such offenses to protect self from being hurt again. It is a self-preservation mechanism that the brain gives instinctive attention to as a means of our survival. The upside of this is that we are better prepared for what might go wrong in life. The downside is that we are prone to keep records of perceived wrongs people have done against us in life. This directly relates to our ability to forgive others, pray for them and believe that they will grow in life. I'm not the person I used to be, are you?

"Bear with each other and forgive one another if any of you has

a grievance against someone. Forgive as the Lord forgave you."
(Colossians 3:13 NIV)

Does not delight in evil but rejoices in the truth: to "not delight in evil" can be seen as not wallowing over someone else's guilt. Our fallen nature rejoices when an enemy is punished for their evil ways or has their sin exposed. This attitude opposes love. Love finds value in every person and recognizes that they are loved by God. We are to rejoice in this truth and pray for our enemies who are the ones in trouble.

"Do good to those who hate you, bless those who curse you, pray for those who abuse you." (Luke 6:27–28)

It always protects: This is an interesting concept, because the Greek word for protect actually means "cover" and includes the idea of protecting and preserving. Protection directly relates to watching out for others and if someone is vulnerable and faltering in some way, love will cover and protect such a one. Love protects is the essence of not seeking one's own way, but caring for others. It reminds me of when Noah had too much to drink and passed out naked in his tent. His one son Ham made fun of it while his two other sons, Shem and Japheth, placed a garment on their shoulders and, going backwards, covered the nakedness of their father (Genesis 9:20-23). This is a sign of true protection. Love will always seek to protect others. If there is a shortcoming or failure in a loved one, love has the ability to cover up strife related to it. Proverbs 10:12 reads, "Hatred stirs up strife, but love covers all offenses." In other words, those who live outside of love will have contempt toward those who stumble, but love will produce mercy and grace to all offenses of others. This is exactly what God's love has done for us, and so much more.

It always trusts: The Greek word used here is *pistis* which translates to believe, faith, confidence, or trust. In many Bible translations, it reads "believes all things" (KJV, ESV, ASV, NKJV, etc.) Yet many scriptures use the word *pistis* to speak of faith such as, "For by grace you have been saved through *faith*; and that not of yourselves, it is the gift of God." (Ephesians 2:8) and in many other faith scriptures (Rom. 12:3, Gal. 5:22, 2 Cor. 8:7, 1 Jn. 5:4) and so on. People have trouble understanding "always trusts" because most people have been hurt by the actions of others and have lost their ability to trust. I consider this as a call to have confidence, believe, and have faith. Trust that God will work all things out for good as we pursue him. The core of our faith is knowing that God is our Father and only has good things in store for us within a troubled world. This is the good news- that we can trust God to always take care of us.

It always hopes: Hope is nothing less than confidence in the reality of God's Kingdom and his promises to us.

"Faith is being sure of what we hope for and certain of what we do not see." (Hebrews 11:1 ESV)

In addition to our hope being manifest in our confidence in God, love is also expressed as hope in our relationships with people, believing the best for them. We can all think of someone who has so much hope for our success in life that we draw strength by simply being around them. This is love that always hopes. Simply put, hope is demonstrated in a positive attitude no matter what comes our way. We can demonstrate this same loving hope to those we are in relationship with, which builds them up in faith. It's one thing to believe in God's affirming hope in us, but such hope is noticeably experienced when we show one another love through hope.

It always perseveres: In some Bible versions, the word "endure" is used, but the intent is the same. Love never gives up despite life's difficulties and challenges. This persevering love is motivated by our love of God and others. It isn't always easy or convenient to persevere or endure through life's circumstances, but Godly love is a commitment to always pursue the highest good for ourselves and others, no matter what obstacles come our way. Part of this also has to do with persevering through persecution. Our old man despises being treated wrongfully, but our new man is to accept persecution without personal concern, but with a focus on God's love. 1 Peter 2:20 tells us, "If you suffer for doing good and you endure it, this is commendable before God." We are to persevere in love during our hardships and persevere in giving love to others throughout their difficulties.

Although this is not an exhaustive study of this passage, suffice it to say that it is in the best interest of every believer to understand the love that is God, which we are called to be.

It's not enough to just know the words of 1 Corinthians 13. We need wisdom and understanding in order to apply it.

"Wisdom is the principle thing; Therefore get wisdom. And in all your getting, get understanding." (Proverbs 4:7)

"If any of you lacks wisdom, let him ask of God, who gives to all liberally and without reproach, and it will be given to him. But let him ask in faith, with no doubting, for he who doubts is like a wave of the sea driven and tossed by the wind." (James 1:5-6)

"Dear children, let us not love with words or speech but with actions and in truth." (1 John 3:18 NIV)

Chapter Twelve

Red Letters

A red-letter Bible has all the words of Jesus printed in the color red. Although I and many other Christians have owned one, most of us have not realized the importance of those red letters. They are there to tell us what Jesus said and thought throughout his earthly life and ministry, giving us insight into what occupied his mind.

When I gave my attention to reading and meditating on the words Jesus spoke, my understanding of his mind was awakened. What he spent his time thinking about was starkly different than what I have spent my time thinking about. This was discouraging, but inspired me to know more about his thoughts.

As I looked at the contrast between my thoughts and those of Christ, all I could say was "ouch." I was overwhelmed by the significance of his thoughts and the spiritual insignificance of mine. Having known and served the Lord for over forty-five years, I felt as if I were starting out all over again.

I was confronted by this thought: is it possible to make such a mental shift? It was as if I was looking up at Mount Everest realizing I needed to climb it to the summit, but with no skills, gear or knowledge of how to get there. Fortunately, this point of view results in deep humility, which is the best starting place when seeking spiritual growth.

Before I share a few of my favorite red-letter passages, I want to say that there is nothing convenient in thinking with the mind of Christ. If we are to think as him, we face the potential of being judged by our families and other believers, and being called to do things that will interrupt our lives and cost us financially, emotionally, and oftentimes circumstantially. To think as Christ, we will also suffer persecution as Christ.

"These things I have spoken to you, that in Me you may have peace. In the world you will have tribulation; but be of good cheer, I have overcome the world." John 16:33

"Beloved, do not think it strange concerning the fiery trial which is to try you, as though some strange thing happened to you; but rejoice to the extent that you partake of Christ's sufferings, that when his glory is revealed, you may also be glad with exceeding joy. (1 Peter 4:12-13)

I have made paragraph breaks within these passages to create mental pauses for reflection.

> But I say to you who hear: Love your enemies, do good to those who hate you, bless those who curse you, and pray for those who spitefully use you. To him who strikes you on the one cheek, offer the other also.

> And from him who takes away your cloak, do not withhold your tunic either. Give to everyone who asks of you. And from anyone who takes away your goods do not ask them back.

> And just as you want men to do to you, you also do to them likewise. But if you love those who love you, what credit is that to you? For even sinner's love those who love them. And if you do good to those who do good to you, what credit is

that to you? For even sinners do the same.

And if you lend to those from whom you hope to receive back, what credit is that to you? For sinners lend to sinners to receive as much back. But love your enemies, do good, and lend, hoping for nothing in return; and your reward will be great, and you will be sons of the Most High. For He is kind to the unthankful and evil.

Therefore be merciful, just as your Father is also merciful. Judge not, and you shall not be judged. Condemn not, and you shall not be condemned. Forgive, and you will be forgiven.

Luke 6:27-37

Have I matured enough in Christ to love my enemies and do good to those who hate me? Am I blessing those who curse me and praying for those who take advantage of me?

How do I react when something is taken from me or stolen from my home? Should I meet such thieves, how do I treat them?

Do I treat people as I want to be treated? Do I love people who I normally would disregard, or avoid them because they irritate me? What is in me that makes me so critical of others?

Am I still lending to others or have I matured to the point of giving to others asking for nothing in return? Do I show kindness to those who are evil, or show kindness to people who are ungrateful?

Do I show mercy to sinners or do I judge them? Do I treat sinners as if there is no hope for them? Is there forgiveness for everyone in my heart?

"Forgiveness is the fragrance that the violet sheds on the heel that has crushed it."   Mark Twain

Do not lay up for yourselves treasures on earth, where moth and rust destroy and where thieves break in and steal; but lay up for yourselves treasures in heaven, where neither moth nor rust destroys and where thieves do not break in and steal. For where your treasure is, there your heart will be also.

The lamp of the body is the eye. If therefore your eye is good, your whole body will be full of light. But if your eye is bad, your whole body will be full of darkness. If therefore the light that is in you is darkness, how great is that darkness! No one can serve two masters; for either he will hate the one and love the other, or else he will be loyal to the one and despise the other. You cannot serve both God and mammon.

Therefore I say to you, do not worry about your life, what you will eat or what you will drink; nor about your body, what you will put on. Is not life more than food and the body more than clothing? Look at the birds of the air, for they neither sow nor reap nor gather into barns yet your heavenly Father feeds them. Are you not of more value than they? Which of you by worrying can add one cubit to his stature? So why do you worry about clothing? Consider the lilies of the field, how they grow: they neither toil nor spin; and yet I say to you that even Solomon in all his glory was not arrayed like one of these. Now if God so clothes the grass of the field, which today is, and tomorrow is thrown into the oven, will He not much more clothe you, O you of little faith?

Therefore do not worry, saying 'What shall we eat?' or 'What shall we drink?' or 'What shall we wear?' For after all these things the Gentiles seek. For your heavenly Father knows that you need all these things. But seek first the kingdom of God and His righteousness, and all these things shall be added to you. Therefore do not worry about tomorrow, for tomorrow will worry about its own things. Sufficient for the day is its own trouble.

Matthew 6:19-34

Am I still attached to material possessions? Does my heart still long for experiences that are of this world?

Is my spiritual eye full of God's light or is it still contaminated by the world's point of view? Am I concerned with worldly affairs? Do I still see money as the power that controls how much enjoyment I get out of this life? What makes me afraid of not having enough money?

Do I still think a lot about tomorrow or worry about what I have to drink, eat or wear? Have I matured enough to think regularly about God's kingdom? Do I look at others as being objects of his love or just as bystanders?

"The gift of salvation is a transformed life." Dan Mohler

When the Son of Man comes in His glory, and all the holy angels with Him, then He will sit on the throne of His glory. All the nations will be gathered before Him, and He will separate them one from another, as a shepherd divides his sheep from the goats. And He will set the sheep on His right hand, but the goats on the left. Then the King will say to those on His right hand, 'Come, you blessed of My Father, inherit the kingdom prepared for you from the foundation of the world: for I was hungry and you gave Me food; I was thirsty and you gave Me drink; I was a stranger and you took Me in; I was naked and you clothed Me; I was sick and you visited Me; I was in prison and you came to Me.'

Then the righteous will answer Him, saying, 'Lord, when did we see You hungry and feed You, or thirsty and give You drink? When did we see You a stranger and take You in, or naked and clothe You? Or when did we see You sick, or in prison, and come to You?' And the King will answer and say to them, 'Assuredly, I say to you, inasmuch as you did it to one of the least of these My brethren, you did it to Me.'

Then He will also say to those on the left hand, 'Depart from Me, you cursed, into the everlasting fire prepared for the devil and his angels: for I was hungry and you gave Me no food; I was thirsty and you gave Me no drink; I was a stranger and you did not take Me in, naked and you did not clothe Me, sick and in prison and you did not visit Me.'

Then they also will answer Him, saying, 'Lord, when did we see You hungry or thirsty or a stranger or naked or sick or in prison, and did not minister to You?' Then He will answer them, saying, 'Assuredly, I say to you, inasmuch as you did not do it to one of the least of these, you did not do it to Me.'

Matthew 25: 31-45

How much am I aware of those who are hungry or thirsty around me? Do I make an effort to provide clothing to those who have so little? When I hear someone is sick, do I make an effort to go and visit them, or am I afraid I'll pick up some germs? If someone I know goes to jail or prison do I go to visit them?

Am I afraid of those who are impoverished, handicapped, or peculiar? Do I fear something bad happening to me or do I completely trust the Lord to protect me from harm?

Be aware that I am specifically pointing out our need to grow so that God can tell us what to say and do. When we obey his instructions, we have nothing to fear. We are not called to be foolish, we are called to know our God and obey him.

"Only a life lived for others is a life worthwhile." Albert Einstein

Have you considered within these verses that Jesus meant what he said? His teachings are as revolutionary today as they were over 2,000 years ago. He introduced mankind to the Kingdom of God, a striking landmark in history. The Old Testament provided us with prophecies about this kingdom (Isaiah 35: 1-4, 8-10, Isaiah 40: 9-11, Jeremiah 23: 3-4, Daniel 2:24, etc.). Yet Jesus came to introduce us to the core value of God's Kingdom, which is unconditional love. He revealed a new way of thinking, behaving and living that was completely foreign to the nature of the descendants of Adam. To fallen man, his teachings were peculiar yet intriguing because they revealed a much deeper spiritual reality than previously known.

The majority of Israel's chief priests, Pharisees, and Sadducees were reduced to the nature of fallen man: pride, scorn, self-righteousness, haughty and a continual pursuance of their own interests to the detriment of God's people. With the coming of the Messiah to deliver man from his Adamic nature by his sacrifice, Jesus Christ revealed the truth that God is love and his Kingdom is ruled by this nature and is not thwarted by evil but overcomes evil with good.

Repay no one evil for evil. Have regard for good things in the sight of all men. If it is possible, as much as depends on you, live peaceably with all men. Beloved, do not avenge yourselves, but rather give place to wrath; for it is written, 'Vengeance is Mine, I will repay,' says the Lord. Therefore 'If your enemy is hungry, feed him; If he is thirsty, give him a drink; For in so doing you will heap coals of fire on his head.' Do not be overcome by evil, but overcome evil with good.

Romans 12:17-21

If we are to experience the mind of Christ, we must embrace his words and live according to what he thought and said. Christ is readily available to help us.

"Whoever says he abides in Him ought to walk in the same way in which He walked." (1 John 2:6)

None of us are there yet, but if we each have this attitude, we will put to death our reactions to criticisms and offenses. And though we may still stumble, we will learn that carrying the cross is not merely dying to self; it is embracing the love of Christ that forgives the very ones who have crucified us, that the battle that comes against us has actually driven us into the embrace of God.

Francis Frangipane

Chapter Thirteen

Now We Die

In reading the gospels, we've all observed how hard it was for the disciples to grasp what Christ was telling them. He spoke revolutionary truths they hadn't heard before. There were many times they were perplexed by what he said and would talk amongst themselves. Christ knew what they were discussing and often resolved their confusion. Yet there were many things they wouldn't understand until after his resurrection.

"These things I have spoken to you while being present with you. But the Helper, the Holy Spirit, whom the Father will send in My name, He will teach you all things, and bring to your remembrance all things that I said to you." (John 14:25-26)

How amazing that we have the Holy Spirit with us from the moment we accept Christ. We have unlimited access to the one who knows all things, yet we are not much different than the disciples.

For as many of the scriptures have told us that we must die to our old selves and be born again into a new life, we have yet to understand the breadth of it. Somehow, many of us have fed at a Christian buffet where we pick and choose what parts of Christianity we want to partake of. Obviously, we want to die to our dishonesty, insecurity, laziness, depression, and pride. Still, many of us have yet to jump at the chance to give up our desires, interests, wants, and will. After all, many things in this world are so appealing to us and are not necessarily bad in and of themselves, or are they?

All such thinking is foolishness when compared to the reality that we are either slaves to the sinful nature and a fallen world, or slaves to righteousness and the kingdom of heaven. The word slave sounds so harsh, but Paul was using it in Romans 6 to help the current culture of people understand what he was saying (Romans 6:19). Perhaps it's more palatable if I say we are either a slave of the Dark Side or the Force, Darth Vader or Yoda. There are only two options. That's it. No pun intended, but being a slave to sin is a dead end. To say it is a bleak existence is a gross understatement.

"And these will go away into everlasting punishment, but the righteous into eternal life." (Matthew 25:46)

If it weren't for God sending Christ to earth, there wouldn't be a second option.

The heavenly Father's desire has always been to restore us to our original form of his love. Christ died so that the penalty for our sins was paid by the shedding of his blood, but this was *in order that* we might know our heavenly Father and be restored to our original purpose. As Jesus said in Matthew 18:11, "For the Son of Man came to save that which was lost." He didn't say to save *those* that were lost, but *that* which was lost- being our original purpose in God.

Only as we take steps to control our thoughts, address wrong attitudes and nourish our spirits in God will we begin to recognize thoughts coming from the mind of Christ within us. Getting to this point is the challenge because denying ourselves is extreme, but everything we were before Christ was a lie. We have not been living in our created purpose, but living according to a fallen world, corrupted by sin. The more we immerse ourselves into the reality of God's kingdom, the easier it gets. As we begin to think like Christ, we no longer have opinions, a reputation, nothing to defend, nothing to prove, no complaints, and are no longer reactionary to life on earth. The world loses its appeal.

We are creatures of God's love for humanity and every encounter with people is an opportunity to tell and/or show them that they are loved by God. We are now compelled to see the value of each person as the object of God's love. When our own desires no longer consume us, it's much easier to take an interest in the needs and concerns of others. It is a wonderful freedom to no longer be obsessed with self.

Where we once found our value in corrupt standards, psychology, human interactions, and the way that seems right to a man (Proverbs 14:12), we now find our value within us, Christ, the hope of glory (Colossians 1:27). It is the expression of his nature from within each person's individuality that brings glory to God. He made each of us unique so that each person's expression of Christ is different, as in the colors of the rainbow. Each beautiful, yet each exceptional. There is *nothing* in this world that compares to the experience of being Christ to others where there is fulness of joy.

The concept of denial to self is foreign to new believers. It's new territory and a new process of discovering the *how* of it. If this is you, start by taking steps to notice wrong attitudes. It's amazing how emotions in our bodies indicate a self-attitude. For instance, experiencing a bristling emotion can be attached to being offended by someone's comment to you that causes a defensive reaction within us. Fortunately, such emotions are red flags that indicate self-centeredness and can be used to address underlying patterns of thought. Freedom from self is available to us as we acknowledge our folly. In truth, heavenly thoughts are filled with creative power that will change us, compared to earthly thoughts that imprison us.

With Christ in us, our value so far exceeds what we could experience apart from him that, should we understand it, we would run headlong after it. As Paul said in Philippians 3:12, "Not that I have already attained, or am already perfected; but I press on, that I lay hold of that for which Christ Jesus has also laid hold of me."

I assure you, by the grace and mercy of our Lord, that once you grasp the truth of your value in God you will understand the word on a whole new level as the Holy Spirit reveals truth to you. The love of God for you is immeasurable.

> ...that Christ may dwell in your hearts through faith; that you, being rooted and grounded in love, may be able to comprehend with all the saints what is the width and length and depth and height- to know the love of Christ which passes knowledge; that you may be filled with all the fullness of God.
>
> Ephesians 3:17-18

"If you then were raised with Christ, seek those things which are above, where Christ is, sitting at the right hand of God. Set your mind on things above, not on things on the earth. For you died, and your life is hidden with Christ in God." (Colossians 3:1-3)

"If anyone desires to come after Me, let him deny himself, and take up his cross, and follow Me. For whoever desires to save his life will lose it, but whoever loses his life for My sake will find it." (Matthew 16:24-25)

> Or do you not know that as many of us as were baptized into Christ Jesus were baptized into his death? Therefore we were buried with Him through baptism into death, that just as Christ was raised from the dead by the glory of the Father, even so we also should walk in newness of life. For if we

have been united together in knowing this, that our old man was crucified with Him, that the body of sin might be done away with, that we should no longer be slaves of sin. For he who has died has been freed from sin. Now if we died with Christ, we believe that we shall also live with Him, knowing that Christ, having been raised from the dead, dies no more. Death no longer has dominion over Him. For the death that he died, He died to sin once for all; but the life that He lives, He lives to God. Likewise you also, reckon yourselves to be dead indeed to sin, but alive to God in Christ Jesus our Lord.

Romans 6:3-11

"If anyone desires to come after me, let him deny himself, and take up his cross, and follow Me. For whoever desires to save His life will lose it, but whoever loses his life for My sake will find it." (Matthew 16: 24-25)

"And whoever does not bear His cross and come after Me cannot be My disciple." (Luke 14:27)

"For to me, to live is Christ, and to die is gain." (Philippians 1:21)

"I have been crucified with Christ; it is no longer I who live, but Christ lives in me; and the life which I now live in the flesh I live by faith in the Son of God, who loved me and gave Himself for me." (Galatians 2:20)

"Owe no one anything except to love one another, for he who loves another has fulfilled the law." (Romans 13:8)

The freedom that comes from living in the love of God is unparalleled. We are no longer bound by the values of life on earth but live to fulfill the call to love. No more judgment, criticism, gossip, or attitudes that make us self-centered and focused on our personal needs being met. We are new creations that are completely cared for by our loving Father. If someone lashes out to hurt us, we no longer take it personally, but can recognize that they are hurting inside. From this approach, we can reach out to them in love, rather than avoiding them. They are no longer our enemies, but just people who need God's love. It's a completely new perspective that changes us dramatically. We can finally see others as Jesus sees them. As Jesus demonstrated for us, love lays down its life for everyone.

"Most assuredly, I say to you, unless a grain of wheat falls into the ground and dies, it remains alone; but if it dies, it produces much grain." (John 12:24)

It's interesting to note that one grain of wheat can produce eight or more heads with over forty seeds per head.

Although Jesus said this as he was quickly approaching his own death and resurrection, it was also speaking to the importance of a believer's own death to self-centeredness being followed by verse 25 which reads, "He who loves his life will lose it, and he who hates his life in this world will keep it for eternal life."

The word "hate" is used for emphasis. Jesus knows it is very difficult to let go of our desire for the things of this world. We have been conformed, squeezed into a mold as it were, to live in a world-driven way. In using the word hate, Christ is pointing out the intensity in which we must give up our way of living and be transformed into a new way of living. He also used the word hate in relation to our family relationships.

"If anyone comes to Me and does not hate his father and mother, wife and children, brothers and sisters, yes, even his own life also, he cannot be My disciple. And whoever does not bear his cross and come after Me cannot be My disciple." (Luke 14:26-27)

This passage is followed by Jesus giving the example of counting the cost before building a tower or a king preparing to go to war. In other words, he was emphasizing the fact that we must be willing to give up everything to be his disciple. Nothing is off limits. Whatever we must sacrifice in order to follow Christ's leading is worth it, no matter how heartbreaking it may seem at the time.

"And everyone who has left houses or brothers of sisters or father or mother or wife or children or lands, for My name's sake, shall receive a hundredfold, and inherit eternal life." (Matthew 19:29)

We are in a continual process of change and it's up to us to be aware of the potential for moment by moment change.

Choose Jesus.

"If you're thinking of becoming a Christian, I warn you, you're embarking on something, which will take the whole of you." (C.S. Lewis)

Chapter Fourteen

Living in the Paradox

Most people don't realize that Jesus was a rabbi. This is something that many have yet to consider. There are plenty of books about Jesus the rabbi available online, or the condensed study through a video found on Shane Willard Ministries website on the Authority of the Rabbi, covering the subject of Jesus' rabbinical authority.

It was the desire of every Hebrew to become a rabbi. The training was quite difficult. Children needed to memorize the book of Leviticus by the age of six (having it recited to them by their father) and then memorize the Torah, the first five books of the Bible called the Pentateuch, by the age of twelve.

Rabbis would weed out the students, only accepting the best of the best students. It was only when a rabbi called one forth with the words "follow me" that a student knew he had passed the test. All others were told to go and learn their fathers' trades as they didn't make the cut.

Jesus studied the scriptures and it took eighteen years, from the age of twelve, to complete the process. This is why Jesus didn't enter ministry until the age of thirty. He was completely immersed in learning the scriptures and becoming a learned rabbi. This was reflected during his time with teachers in the temple courts at age twelve, asking and answering spiritual questions to their amazement (Luke 2: 41-52).

The most advanced rabbis received a position of power, enabling them to create their own philosophical approach to the scriptures which was called their "yoke." Jesus was one such rabbi, which is why he told us in the scriptures, "Come to me, all you who are weary and burdened, and I will give you rest. Take my yoke upon you and learn from me, for I am gentle and humble in heart, and you will find rest for your souls. For my yoke is easy and my burden is light." (Matthew 11: 28-30)

In this passage, we can all relate to being weary and burdened just by the cares of this life, but how much greater the burden for those trying to fulfill the requirements of the Old Testament laws. Christ promises to give rest to all that will come to him. His call was to take his "yoke" and learn his interpretation of scriptures for he is gentle and humble in heart. Christ then repeats that, in doing so, you will find rest for your souls.

Jesus referred to his yoke, or philosophy, as being "easy" for it was based on love, mercy, and grace, rather than the burden of the religious regulations.   His teachings offended the leaders of that day, as it stripped them of power to lord over their subjects. His yoke comes from a position of rest: resting in the ultimate forgiveness of God provided through the sacrifice of his only Son; resting from the critical and harsh judgment of the Covenant of Law, accepting and loving sinners as they are the recipients of God's mercy and grace.

The fact that Jesus was a rabbi is quite important. Since rabbis chose the best students by telling them "follow me," it makes it all the more important that Jesus called his disciples in such a way, despite the fact that they didn't make the cut. They understood what he was saying to them and jumped at the opportunity to follow this rabbi.

As Jesus taught his disciples about his yoke, it was completely different than the yokes of the other rabbis. He was gentle and humble. He confronted the scribes and Pharisees for their self-righteousness and confronted their elitist attitudes and prideful arrogance. He was not driven to display his rightful authority because he came to show the tender kindness and love of God for humanity.

His yoke was designed to make it possible to effectively live our lives in the way God originally designed them to be lived, in unconditional love. It doesn't relieve us of the burdens of life, but we now have a way called "love" that overcomes the carnal world we live in. As Christ himself said in John 16:33, "These things I have spoken to you, that in Me you may have peace. In the world you will have tribulation; but be of good cheer, I have overcome the world."

When Jesus calls us to "follow," it is much more than being a Christian, but becoming one of his students that he wants to communicate with intimately. It is, in fact, a summoning of miraculous proportions. As we've been learning, to follow Jesus is an *all or nothing* summons that affects every area of our lives. If we don't give up all we have to Jesus, we will lose all in the end.

Ultimately, the life that we are to live in Christ is in complete opposition to our earthly system. We are called to live in a paradox, contradicting earthly norms. The teachings of Jesus were contrary to the ways of the world. His Sermon on the Mount, known as The Beatitudes, reveals how different his teachings were from current thinking.

> Blessed are the poor in spirit, For theirs is the kingdom of heaven. Blessed are those who mourn, for they shall be comforted. Blessed are the meek, for they shall inherit the earth. Blessed are those who hunger and thirst for righteousness, For they shall be filled. Blessed are the merciful, for they shall obtain mercy. Blessed are the pure in

heart, For they shall see God. Blessed are the peacemakers, for they shall be called the sons of God. Blessed are those who are persecuted for righteousness' sake, For theirs is the kingdom of heaven. Blessed are you when they revile and persecute you, and say all kinds of evil against you falsely for My sake. Rejoice and be exceedingly glad, for great is your reward in heaven, for so they persecuted the prophets who were before you.

Matthew 5:3-12

Particularly in this period of the Roman empire, none of those whom he called blessed were valued. They were scoffed at as being weak and pathetic. Although in this generation there is an affinity to perform random acts of kindness and generosity, they are driven by the desire for experiencing self-worth.

Paul pointed out the severity of our paradoxes.

…by honor and dishonor, by evil report and good report; as deceivers, and yet true; as unknown, and yet well known; as dying, and behold we live; as chastened, and yet not killed; as sorrowful, yet always rejoicing; as poor, yet making many rich; as having nothing, and yet possessing all things.

2 Corinthians 6:8-10

Continuing his theme, if we want to be great, we must serve everyone; if we want to be exalted, we must be humble; we only become free when we become God's bondservants; to gain rest, we must put on a yoke. God's strength resides in our weakness. We receive when we give, and true living is acquired through dying.

"Behold what manner of love the Father has bestowed on us, that we should be called children of God! Therefore the world does not know us, because it did not know Him." (1 John 3:1)

"Blessed be the God and Father of our Lord Jesus Christ, who has blessed us with every spiritual blessing in the heavenly places in Christ." (Ephesians 1:3)

> Now, therefore, you are no longer strangers and foreigners, but fellow citizens with the saints and members of the household of God, having been built on the foundation of the apostles and prophets, Jesus Christ Himself being the chief cornerstone, in whom the whole building, being fitted together, grows into a holy temple in the Lord, in whom you also are being built together for a dwelling place of God in the Spirit.
>
> Ephesians 2:19-22

"If you want a religion to make you feel really comfortable, I certainly don't recommend Christianity." (C.S. Lewis)

Experiencing the Mind of Christ Journal

When I completed the book Experiencing the Mind of Christ, I realized I needed to use it as a guide for myself to move more deeply into thinking like Christ. I started a workbook where I had topics from the book that I could meditate on. As I reflected on my own patterns of thought, I recognized things that kept me preoccupied with the world, rather than the things of heaven. Ultimately, it became more of a journal as I found the Lord teaching me more about what I should think about which became quite helpful. I decided to put together this journal for those of you who would like some help moving forward in your journey to experience the mind of Christ.

Even though we know that all sinful worldly thoughts and traits are destroyed by the word of God, we don't often take the time to seek the scriptures regarding our struggles. In this technological era, all one has to do is enter a Google search such as "scriptures about fear" and there will appear a large choice of scriptures to speak against fear. Write down your findings and speak them aloud on a regular basis, for they are life-giving.

May the Lord overtake you with His eternal love as you pursue to know Him better.

Theresa Cummings

Colossians 3:23-24 New King James Version (NKJV)
"And whatever you do, do it heartily, as to the Lord and not to men, knowing that from the Lord you will receive the reward of the inheritance; for you serve the Lord Christ."

CAPTURED THOUGHTS...

What are some thoughts from my past that trouble me?

_____

_____

_____

_____

_____

_____

_____

_____

_____

_____

_____

_____

_____

_____

_____

_____

What events in my past reflect God's faithfulness to me?

_____

_____

_____

_____

_____

_____

_____

_____

_____

_____

_____

_____

_____

_____

_____

_____

What thoughts do I have about my future that preoccupy my mind?

_____

_____

_____

_____

_____

_____

_____

_____

_____

_____

_____

_____

_____

_____

_____

_____

What scriptures will help me have security about my future?

_____

_____

_____

_____

_____

_____

_____

_____

_____

_____

_____

_____

_____

_____

_____

_____

What thoughts do I have that bring up sadness, or negative emotions?

_____

_____

_____

_____

_____

_____

_____

_____

_____

_____

_____

_____

_____

_____

What scriptures help me experience the joy of the Lord?

_____

_____

_____

_____

_____

_____

_____

_____

_____

_____

_____

_____

_____

_____

_____

What thoughts do I have that create fear in me?

_____

_____

_____

_____

_____

_____

_____

_____

_____

_____

_____

_____

_____

_____

_____

_____

What scriptures can I proclaim to destroy those fears?

_____

_____

_____

_____

_____

_____

_____

_____

_____

_____

_____

_____

_____

_____

_____

_____

What thoughts do I have that cause me to doubt God and His promises to me?

_____

_____

_____

_____

_____

_____

_____

_____

_____

_____

_____

_____

_____

_____

_____

What scriptures about faith will overcome all doubt?

_____

_____

_____

_____

_____

_____

_____

_____

_____

_____

_____

_____

_____

_____

_____

_____

What thoughts do I have that make me angry?

_____

_____

_____

_____

_____

_____

_____

_____

_____

_____

_____

_____

_____

_____

_____

_____

_____

What scriptures can help me deal with my anger properly?

_____

_____

_____

_____

_____

_____

_____

_____

_____

_____

_____

_____

_____

_____

_____

_____

What thoughts do I have that make me feel jealous of others?

_____

_____

_____

_____

_____

_____

_____

_____

_____

_____

_____

_____

_____

_____

_____

_____

_____

What thoughts leave me feeling discontent or unsatisfied with my life?

_____

_____

_____

_____

_____

_____

_____

_____

_____

_____

_____

_____

_____

_____

_____

What scriptures create peace and satisfaction in me no matter what my circumstances are?

_____

_____

_____

_____

_____

_____

_____

_____

_____

_____

_____

_____

_____

_____

_____

Philippians 4:8 tells us what to think about in order to be heavenly minded. Write down what can you think about regarding each item the Apostle Paul mentioned. What can I think about that is ...

True

_____

_____

_____

_____

_____

_____

_____

_____

_____

_____

_____

_____

_____

Honest

140

Just

_____
_____
_____
_____
_____
_____
_____
_____
_____
_____
_____
_____
_____
_____
_____
_____

Pure

_____

_____

_____

_____

_____

_____

_____

_____

_____

_____

_____

_____

_____

_____

_____

_____

_____

Lovely

_____

_____

_____

_____

_____

_____

_____

_____

_____

_____

_____

_____

_____

_____

_____

_____

_____

Good News

_____

_____

_____

_____

_____

_____

_____

_____

_____

_____

_____

_____

_____

_____

_____

_____

_____

_____

144

Virtuous and Righteous

_____

_____

_____

_____

_____

_____

_____

_____

_____

_____

_____

_____

_____

_____

_____

_____

_____

_____

Worthy of Praise

_____

_____

_____

_____

_____

_____

_____

_____

_____

_____

_____

_____

_____

_____

_____

_____

_____

_____

Three things we are encouraged to give our attention to in 1 Thessalonians 5:16-18: joy, prayer, and gratitude. On any given day, write down your experience with each.

Joy

_____

_____

_____

_____

_____

_____

_____

_____

_____

_____

_____

_____

_____

Prayer

Gratitude

_____

_____

_____

_____

_____

_____

_____

_____

_____

_____

_____

_____

_____

_____

_____

_____

What did I speak today that was life-giving?

_____

_____

_____

_____

_____

_____

_____

_____

_____

_____

_____

_____

_____

_____

_____

What did I speak today that was unkind or negative?

_____

_____

_____

_____

_____

_____

_____

_____

_____

_____

_____

_____

_____

_____

_____

Did I walk in humility today?

_____

_____

_____

_____

_____

_____

_____

_____

_____

_____

_____

_____

_____

_____

_____

_____

_____

Did I spend time in worship today?

_____

_____

_____

_____

_____

_____

_____

_____

_____

_____

_____

_____

_____

_____

_____

Did I spend time alone with God today and talk to Him from my heart?

_____

_____

_____

_____

_____

_____

_____

_____

_____

_____

_____

_____

_____

_____

154

What did I learn from God's word today?

_____

_____

_____

_____

_____

_____

_____

_____

_____

_____

_____

_____

_____

_____

_____

In reading 1 Corinthians 13: 4-8, what do I need to do to be more loving?

_____

_____

_____

_____

_____

_____

_____

_____

_____

_____

_____

_____

_____

_____

_____

In 2 Peter 1: 5-11 the Apostle Peter tells me what I need to add to my life to grow in my faith. Where am I weak in these attributes and what can I do to strengthen them?

_____

_____

_____

_____

_____

_____

_____

_____

_____

_____

_____

_____

_____

_____

Additional Personal Notes

CPSIA information can be obtained
at www.ICGtesting.com
Printed in the USA
FSHW010334250120
66224FS